HOME-LIFE OF THE LANCASHIRE FACTORY FOLK

DURING THE COTTON FAMINE

BY

EDWIN WAUGH

ISBN-13:978-1977966087

Author of "Lancashire Sketches", "Poems and Lancashire Songs", "Tufts of Heather from the Northern Moors", etc, etc.

"Hopdance cries in poor Tom's belly for two white herrings. Croak not, black angel:

I have no food for thee." --King Lear.

Cover Image: LS Lowry

PREFACE

The following chapters are reprinted from the columns of the Manchester Examiner and Times, to which Paper they were contributed by the Author during the year 1862. HOME LIFE OF THE LANCASHIRE FACTORY FOLK DURING THE COTTON FAMINE. (Reprinted from the Manchester Examiner and Times of 1862)

CHAPTER I.

AMONG THE BLACKBURN OPERATIVES "Poor Tom's a-cold. Who gives anything to poor Tom?" --King Lear.

Blackburn is one of the towns which has suffered more than the rest in the present crisis, and yet a stranger to the place would not see anything in its outward appearance indicative of this adverse nip of the times. But to any one familiar with the town in its prosperity, the first glance shows that there is now something different on foot there, as it did to me on Friday last. The morning was wet and raw, a state of weather in which Blackburn does not wear an Arcadian aspect, when trade is good. Looking round from the front of the railway station, the first thing which struck me was the great number of tall chimneys which were smokeless, and the unusual clearness of the air. Compared with the appearance of the town when in full activity, there is now a look of doleful holiday, an unnatural fast-day quietness about everything. There were few carts astir, and not so many people in the streets as usual, although so many are out of work there. Several, in the garb of factory operatives, were leaning upon the bridge, and others were trailing along in twos and threes, looking listless and cold; but nobody seemed in a hurry. Very little of the old briskness was visible. When the mills are in full work, the streets are busy with heavy loads of twist and cloth; and the workpeople hurry in blithe crowds to and from the factories, full of life and glee, for factory labour is not so hurtful to healthy life as it was thirty years ago, nor as some people think it now, who don't know much about it. There were few people at the shop windows, and fewer inside. I went into some of the shops to buy trifling things of different kinds, making inquiries about the state of trade meanwhile, and, wherever I went, I met with the same gloomy answers. They were doing nothing, taking nothing; and they didn't know how things would end. They had the usual expenses going on, with increasing rates, and a fearfully lessened income, still growing less. And yet they durst not complain; but had to contribute towards the relief of their starving neighbours, sometimes even when they themselves ought to be receiving relief, if their true condition was known. I heard of several shopkeepers who had not taken more across their counters for weeks past than would pay their rents, and some were not doing even so much as that. This is one painful bit of the kernel of life in Blackburn just now, which is concealed by the quiet shell of outward appearance. Beyond this unusual quietness, a stranger will not see much of the pinch of the times, unless he goes deeper; for the people of Lancashire never were remarkable for hawking their troubles much about the world. In the present untoward pass, their deportment, as a whole, has been worthy of themselves, and their wants have been worthily met by their own neighbours. What it may become necessary to do hereafter, does not yet appear. It is a calamity arising, partly from a wise national forbearance, which will repay itself richly in the long run. But, apart from that wide- spread poverty which is already known and relieved, there is, in times like the present, always a certain small proportion, even of the poorest, who will "eat their cake to th' edge," and then starve bitterly before they will complain. These are the flower of our working population; they are of finer stuff than the common staple of human nature. Amongst such there must be many touching cases of distress which do not come to light, even by accident. If they did, nobody can doubt the existence of a generous will to relieve them generously. To meet such cases, it is pleasant to learn, however, as I did, that there is a large amount of private benevolence at work in Blackburn, industriously searching out the most deserving cases of distress. Of course, this kind of benevolence never gets into the statistics of relief, but it will not the less meet with its reward. I heard also of one or two wealthy men whose names do not appear as contributors to the public relief fund, who have preferred to spend considerable sums of money in this private way. In my wanderings about the town I heard also of several instances of poor people holding relief tickets, who, upon meeting with some temporary employment, have returned their tickets to the committee for the benefit of those less fortunate than themselves. Waiving for the present all mention of the opposite picture; these things are alike honourable to both rich and poor.

A little past noon, on Friday, I set out to visit the great stone quarries on the southern edge of the town, where upwards of six hundred of the more robust factory operatives are employed in the lighter work of the quarries. This labour consists principally of breaking up the small stone found in the facings of the solid rock, for the purpose of road-mending and the like. Some, also, are employed in agricultural work, on the ground belonging to the fine new workhouse there. These factory operatives, at the workhouse grounds, and in the quarries, are paid one shilling a day--not much, but much better than the bread of idleness; and for the most part, the men like it better, I am told. The first quarry I walked into was the one known by the name of "Hacking's Shorrock Delph." There I sauntered about, looking at the scene. It was not difficult to distinguish the trained quarrymen from the rest. The latter did not seem to be working very hard at their new employment, and it can hardly be expected that they should, considering the great difference between it and their usual labour. Leaning on their spades and hammers, they watched me with a natural curiosity, as if wondering whether I was a new ganger, or a contractor come to buy stone. There were men of all ages amongst them, from about eighteen years old to white-headed men past sixty. Most of them looked healthy and a little embrowned by recent exposure to the weather; and here and there was a pinched face which told its own tale. I got into talk with a quiet, hardy-looking man, dressed in soil-stained corduroy. He was a kind of overlooker. He told me that there were from eighty to ninety factory hands employed in that quarry. "But," said he, "it varies a bit, yo known. Some on 'em gets knocked up neaw an' then, an' they han to stop a-whoam a day or two; an' some on 'em connot ston gettin' weet through--it mays 'em ill; an' here an' theer one turns up at doesn't like the job at o'--they'd rayther clem. There is at's both willin' an' able; thoose are likely to get a better job, somewheer. There's othersome at's willin' enough, but connot ston th' racket. They dun middlin', tak 'em one wi' another, an' considerin' that they're noan use't to th' wark. Th' hommer fo's leet wi' 'em; but we dunnot like to push 'em so mich, yo known--for what's a shillin' a day? Aw know some odd uns i' this delph at never tastes fro mornin' till they'n done at neet,--an' says nought abeawt it, noather. But they'n families. Beside, fro wake lads, sick as yon, at's bin train't to nought but leet wark, an' a warm place to wortch in, what con yo expect? We'n had a deeal o' bother wi 'em abeawt bein' paid for weet days, when they couldn't wortch. They wur not paid for weet days at th' furst; an' they geet it into their yeds at Shorrock were to blame. Shorrock's th' paymaister, under th' Guardians, But, then, he nobbut went accordin' to orders, yo known. At last, th' Board sattle't that they mut be paid for weet and dry,--an' there's bin quietness sin'. They wortchen fro eight till five; an', sometimes, when they'n done, they drilln o' together i'th road yon--just like sodiurs--an' then they walken away i' procession. But stop a bit;--just go in yon, an' aw'll come to yo in a two-thre minutes." He returned, accompanied by the paymaster, who offered to conduct me through the other delphs. Running over his pay-book, he showed me, by figures opposite each man's name, that, with not more than a dozen exceptions, they had all families of children, ranging in number from two to nine. He then pointed out the way over a knoll, to the next quarry, which is called "Hacking's Gillies' Delph," saying that he would follow me thither. I walked on, stopping for him on the nearest edge of the quarry, which commanded a full view of the men below. They seemed to be waiting very hard for something just then, and they stared at me, as the rest had done; but in a few minutes, just as I began to hear the paymaster's footsteps behind me, the man at the nearest end of the quarry called "Shorrock!" and a sudden activity woke up along the line. Shorrock then pointed to a corner of the delph where two of these poor fellows had been killed the week before, by stones thrown out from a fall of earth. We went down through the delph, and up the slope, by the place where the older men were at work in the poorhouse grounds. Crossing the Darwen road, we passed the other delphs, where the scene was much the same as in the rest, except that more men were employed there. As we went on, one poor fellow was trolling a snatch of song, as he hammered away at the stones. "Thir't merry, owd mon," said I, in passing. "Well," replied he, "cryin' 'll do nought, wilt?" And then, as I walked away, he shouted after me, with a sort of sad smile, "It's a poor heart at never rejoices, maister." Leaving the quarries, we waited below, until the men had struck work for the day, and the whole six hundred came trooping down the road, looking hard at me as they went by, and stopping here and there, in whispering groups. The paymaster told me that one-half of the men's wages was paid to them in tickets for bread--in each case given to the shopkeeper to whom the receiver of the ticket owed most money-- the other half was paid to them in money every Saturday. Before returning to town I learnt that twenty of the more robust men, who had worked well for their shilling a day in the quarries, had been picked out by order of the Board of Guardians, to be sent to the scene of the late disaster, in Lincolnshire, where employment had been obtained for them, at the rate of 3s. 4d. per day. They were to muster at six o'clock next morning to breakfast at the soup kitchen, after which they were to leave town by the seven o'clock train. I resolved to be up and see them off. On retiring to bed at the "Old Bull," a good-tempered fellow, known by the name of "Stockings," from the fact of his being "under-boots," promised to waken me by six o'clock; and so I ended the day, after watching "Stockings" write "18" on the soles of my boots, with a lump of chalk.

"Stockings" might as well have kept his bed on Saturday morning. My room was close to the ancient tower, left standing in the parish churchyard; and, at five o'clock, the beautiful bells of St Marie's struck up, filling my little chamber with that heart-stirring music, which, as somebody has well said, "sounds like a voice from the middle ages." I could not make out what all this early melody meant; for I had forgotten that it was the Queen's birthday. The old tower was in full view from my bed, and I lay there a while looking at it, and listening to the bells, and dreaming of Whalley Abbey, and of old features of life in picturesque Blackburnshire, now passed away. I felt no more inclination for sleep; and when the knock came to my door, I was dressed and ready. There were more people in the streets than I expected, and the bells were still ringing merrily. I found the soup kitchen a lively scene. The twenty men were busy at breakfast, and there was a crowd waiting outside to see them off. There were several members of the committee in the kitchen, and amongst them the Rev. Joseph V. Meaney, Catholic priest, went to and fro in cheerful chat. After breakfast, each man received four pounds of bread and one pound of cheese for the day's consumption. In addition to this, each man received one shilling; to which a certain active member of the committee added threepence in each case. Another member of the committee then handed a letter to each of the only three or four out of the twenty who were able to write, desiring each man to write back to the committee,-- not all at once, but on different days, after their arrival. After this, he addressed them in the following words:--"Now, I hope that every man will conduct himself so as to be a credit to himself and an honour to Blackburn. This work may not prove to be such as you will like, and you must not expect it to be so. But, do your best; and, if you find that there is any chance of employment for more men of the same class as yourselves, you must write and let us know, so as to relieve the distress of others who are left behind you. There will be people waiting to meet you before you get to your journey's end; and, I have no doubt, you will meet with every fair encouragement. One-half of your wages will be paid over to each man there; the other half will be forwarded here, for the benefit of your families, as you all know. Now go, and do your duty to the best of your power, and you will never regret it. I wish you all success." At half-past six the men left the kitchen for the station. I lingered behind to get a basin of the soup, which I relished mightily. At the station I found a crowd of wives, children, and friends of those who were going away. Amongst the rest, Dr Rushton, the vicar of Blackburn, and his lady, had come to see them off. Here a sweet little young wife stood on the edge of the platform, with a pretty bareheaded child in her arms, crying as if her heart would break. Her husband now and then spoke a consoling word to her from the carriage window. They had been noticed sharing their breakfast together at the kitchen. A little farther on, a poor old Irishwoman was weeping bitterly. The Rev. Mr Meaney went up to her, and said, "Now, Mrs Davis, I thought you had more sense than to cry." "Oh," said a young Irishwoman, standing beside her, "sure, she's losin' her son from her." "Well," said the clergyman, cheeringly, "it's not your husband, woman." "Ah, thin," replied the young woman, "sure, it's all she has left of him." On the door of one compartment of the carriage there was the following written label:--"Fragile, with care." " How's this, Dennis?" said the Catholic priest to a young fellow nearest the door; "I suppose it's because you're all Irishmen inside there." In another compartment the lads kept popping their heads out, one after another, shouting farewells to their relatives and friends, after which they struck up, "There's a good time coming!" One wag of a fellow suddenly called out to his wife on the platform, "Aw say, Molly, just run for thoose tother breeches o' mine. They'n come in rarely for weet weather." One of his companions replied, "Thae knows hoo cannot get 'em, Jack. Th' pop-shops are noan oppen yet." One hearty cheer arose as the train started, after which the crowd dribbled away from the platform. I returned to the soup kitchen, where the wives, children, and mothers of the men who had gone were at breakfast in the inner compartment of the kitchen. On the outer side of the partition five or six pinched-looking men had straggled in to get their morning meal.

When they had all done but one, who was left reared against the wooden partition finishing his soup, the last of those going away turned round and said, "Sam, theaw'rt noan as tickle abeawt thi mate as thae use't to be." "Naw," replied the other, "it'll not do to be nice these times, owd mon. But, thae use't to think thisel' aboon porritch, too, Jone. Aw'll shake honds wi' tho i' thae's a mind, owd dog." "Get forrud wi' that stuff, an' say nought," answered Jone. I left Sam at his soup, and went up into the town. In the course of the day I sat some hours in the Boardroom, listening to the relief cases; but of this, and other things, I will say more in my next.

CHAPTER II.

A little after ten o'clock on Saturday forenoon, I went into the Boardroom, in the hope of catching there some glimpses of the real state of the poor in Blackburn just now, and I was not disappointed; for amongst the short, sad complainings of those who may always be heard of in such a place, there was many a case presented itself which gave affecting proof of the pressure of the times. Although it is not here where one must look for the most enduring and unobtrusive of those who suffer; nor for the poor traders, who cannot afford to wear their distress upon their sleeves, so long as things will hold together with them at all; nor for that rare class which is now living upon the savings of past labour--yet, there were many persons, belonging to one or other of these classes, who applied for relief evidently because they had been driven unwillingly to this last bitter haven by a stress of weather which they could not bide any longer. There was a large attendance of the guardians; and they certainly evinced a strong wish to inquire carefully into each case, and to relieve every case of real need. The rate of relief given is this (as you will have seen stated by Mr Farnall elsewhere):--"To single able bodied men, 3s. for three days' work. To the man who had a wife and two children, 6s. for six days' work, and he would have 2s. 6d. added to the 6s., and perhaps a pair of clogs for one of his children. To a man who had a wife and four children, 10s. was paid for six days' labour, and in addition 4s., and sometimes 4s. 6d., was given to him, and also bits of clothing and other things which he absolutely wanted." Sitting at that Board I saw some curious--some painful things. It was, as one of the Board said to me, "Hard work being there." In one case, a poor, pale, clean-looking, and almost speechless woman presented herself. Her thin and sunken eyes, as well as her known circumstances, explained her want sufficiently, and I heard one of the guardians whisper to another, "That's a bad case. If it wasn't for private charity they'd die of starvation." "Yes," replied another; "that woman's punished, I can see." Now and then a case came on in which the guardians were surprised to see a man ask for relief whom everybody had supposed to be in good circumstances. The first applicant, after I entered the room, was a man apparently under forty years of age, a beerhouse keeper, who had been comparatively well off until lately. The tide of trouble had whelmed him over. His children were all factory operatives, and all out of work; and his wife was ill. "What; are you here, John?" said the chairman to a decent-looking man who stepped up in answer to his name. The poor fellow blushed with evident pain, and faltered out his story in few and simple words, as if ashamed that anything on earth should have driven him at last to such an extremity as this. In another case, a clean old decrepid man presented himself. "What's brought you here, Joseph?" said the chairman. "Why; aw've nought to do,--nor nought to tak to." "What's your daughter, Ellen, doing, Joseph?" "Hoo's eawt o' wark." "And what's your wife doing?" "Hoo's bin bed-fast aboon five year." The old man was relieved at once; but, as he walked away, he looked hard at his ticket, as if it wasn't exactly the kind of thing; and, turning round, he said, "Couldn't yo let me be a sweeper i'th streets, istid, Mr Eccles?" A clean old woman came up, with a snow- white nightcap on her head. "Well, Mary; what do you want?" "Aw could like yo to gi mo a bit o' summat, Mr Eccles,--for aw need it" "Well, but you've some lodgers, haven't you, Mary?" "Yigh; aw've three." "Well; what do they pay you?" "They pay'n mo nought. They'n no wark,--an' one connot turn 'em eawt."

This was all quite true. "Well, but you live with your son; don't you?" continued the chairman. "Nay," replied the old woman, "HE lives wi' ME; an' he's eawt o' wark, too. Aw could like yo to do a bit o' summat for us. We're hard put to 't." "Don't you think she would be better in the workhouse?" said one of the guardians. "Oh, no," replied another; "don't send th' owd woman there. Let her keep her own little place together, if she can." Another old woman presented herself, with a threadbare shawl drawn closely round her gray head. "Well, Ann," said the chairman, "there's nobody but yourself and your John, is there?" "Nawe." "What age are you?" "Aw'm seventy." "Seventy!" "Aye, I am." "Well, and what age is your John?" "He's gooin' i' seventy-four." "Where is he, Ann ?" "Well, aw laft him deawn i' th' street yon; gettin' a load o' coals in." There was a murmur of approbation around the Board; and the old woman was sent away relieved and thankful. There were many other affecting cases of genuine distress arising from the present temporary severity of the times. Several applicants were refused relief on its being proved that they were already in receipt of considerably more income than the usual amount allowed by the Board to those who have nothing to depend upon. Of course there are always some who, having lost that fine edge of feeling to which this kind of relief is revolting, are not unwilling to live idly upon the rates as much and as long as possible at any time, and who will even descend to pitiful schemes to wring from this source whatever miserable income they can get. There are some, even, with whom this state of mind seems almost hereditary; and these will not be slow to take advantage of the present state of affairs. Such cases, however, are not numerous among the people of Lancashire. It was a curious thing to see the different demeanours and appearances of the applicants--curious to hear the little stories of their different troubles. There were three or four women whose husbands were away in the militia; others whose husbands had wandered away in search of work weeks ago, and had never been heard of, since. There were a few very fine, intelligent countenances among them. There were many of all ages, clean in person, and bashful in manner, with their poor clothing put into the tidiest possible trim; others were dirty, and sluttish, and noisy of speech, as in the case of one woman, who, after receiving her ticket for relief, partly in money and partly in kind, whipped a pair of worn clogs from under her shawl, and cried out, "Aw mun ha' some clogs afore aw go, too; look at thoose! They're a shame to be sin!" Clogs were freely given; and, in several cases, they were all that were asked for. In three or four instances, the applicants said, after receiving other relief, "Aw wish yo'd gi' me a pair o' clogs, Mr Eccles. Aw've had to borrow these to come in." One woman pleaded hard for two pair, saying, "Yon chylt's bar-fuut; an' HE'S witchod (wet-shod), an' as ill as he con be." "Who's witchod?" asked the chairman. "My husban' is," replied the woman; "an' he connot ston it just neaw, yo mun let HIM have a pair iv yo con." "Give her two pairs of clogs," said the chairman. Another woman took her clog off, and held it up, saying,

"Look at that. We're o' walkin' o'th floor; an' smoor't wi' cowds." One decent-looking old body, with a starved face, applied. The chairman said, "Why, what's your son doing now? Has he catched no rabbits lately?" "Nay, aw dunnot know 'at he does. Aw get nought; an' it's ME at wants summat, Mr Eccles," replied the old woman, in a tremulous tone, with the water rising in her eyes. "Well, come; we mustn't punish th' owd woman for her son," said one of the guardians. Various forms of the feebleness of age appeared before the Board that day. "What's your son John getting, Mary?" said the chairman to one old woman. "Whor?" replied she. "What's your son John getting?" The old woman put her hand up to her ear, and answered,

"Aw'm rayther deaf. What say'n yo?" It turned out that her son was taken ill, and they were relieved. In the course of inquiries I found that the working people of Blackburn, as elsewhere in Lancashire, nickname their workshops as well as themselves. The chairman asked a girl where she worked at last, and the girl replied, "At th' 'Puff-an'-dart.'" "And what made you leave there?" "Whau, they were woven up." One poor, pale fellow, a widower, said he had "worched" a bit at "Bang-the-nation," till he was taken ill, and then they had "shopped his place," that is, they had given his work to somebody else. Another, when asked where he had been working, replied, "At Se'nacre Bruck (Seven-acre Brook), wheer th' wild monkey were catched." It seems that an ourang-outang which once escaped from some travelling menagerie, was re-taken at this place. I sat until the last application had been disposed of, which was about half-past two in the afternoon. The business had taken up nearly four hours and a half.

I had a good deal of conversation with people who were intimately acquainted with the town and its people; and I was informed that, in spite of the struggle for existence which is now going on, and not unlikely to continue for some time, there are things happening amongst the working people there, which do not seem wise, under existing circumstances. The people are much better informed now than they were twenty years ago; but, still, something of the old blindness lingers amongst them, here and there. For instance, at one mill, in Blackburn, where the operatives were receiving 11s. a week for two looms, the proprietor offered to give his workpeople three looms each, with a guarantee for constant employment until the end of next August, if they would accept one and a quarter pence less for the weaving of each piece. This offer, if taken, would have raised their wages to an average of 14s. 6d. a week. It was declined, however, and they are now working, as before, only on two looms each, with uncertainty of employment, at 11s. a week. Perhaps it is too much to expect that such things should die out all at once. But I heard also that the bricklayers' labourers at Blackburn struck work last week for an advance of wages from 3s. 6d. a day to 4s. a day. This seems very untimely, to say the least of it. Apart from these things, there is, amongst all classes, a kind of cheery faith in the return of good times, although nobody can see what they may have to go through yet, before the clouds break. It is a fact that there are more than forty new places ready, or nearly ready, for starting, in and about Blackburn, when trade revives.

After dinner, I walked down Darwen Street. Stopping to look at a music-seller's window, a rough-looking fellow, bareheaded and without coat, came sauntering across the road from a shop opposite. As he came near he shouted out, "Nea then Heaw go!" I turned round; and, seeing that I was a stranger, he said, "Oh; aw thought it had bin another chap." "Well," said I, "heaw are yo gettin' on, these times?" "Divulish ill," replied he. "Th' little maisters are runnin' a bit, some three, some four days. T'other are stopt o' together, welly. . . . It's thin pikein' for poor folk just neaw. But th' shopkeepers an' th' ale-heawses are in for it as ill as ony mak. There'll be crashin' amung some on 'em afore lung." After this, I spent a few minutes in the market-place, which was "slacker" than usual, as might be expected, for, as the Scotch proverb says, "Sillerless folk gang fast through the market." Later on, I went up to Bank Top, on the eastern edge of the town, where many factory operatives reside. Of course, there is not any special quarter where they are clustered in such a manner as to show their condition as a whole. They are scattered all round the town, living as near as possible to the mills in which they are employed. Here I talked with some of the small shopkeepers, and found them all more or less troubled with the same complaint. One owner of a provision shop said to me, "Wi'n a deeal o' brass owin'; but it's mostly owin' by folk at'll pay sometime. An' then, th' part on 'em are doin' a bit yo known; an' they bring'n their trifle o' ready brass to us; an' so we're trailin' on. But folk han to trust us a bit for their stuff, dunnot yo see,--or else it would be 'Wo-up!' soon." I heard of one beerhouse, the owner of which had only drawn 1s. 6d. during a whole week. His children were all factory operatives, and all out of work. They were very badly off, and would have been very glad of a few soup tickets; but, as the man said, "Who'd believe me if aw were to go an' ax for relief?" I was told of two young fellows, unemployed factory hands, meeting one day, when one said to the other, "Thae favvurs hungry, Jone." "Nay, aw's do yet, for that," replied Jone. "Well," continued the other; "keep thi heart eawt of thi clogs, iv thi breeches dun eawt-thrive thi carcass a bit, owd lad." "Aye," said Jone, "but what mun I do when my clogs gi'n way?" "Whaw, thae mun go to th' Guardians; they'n gi tho a pair in a minute." "Nay, by __," replied Jone, "aw'll dee furst!"

In the evening, I ran down to the beautiful suburb called Pleasington, in the hope of meeting a friend of mine there; not finding him, I came away by the eight o'clock train. The evening was splendid, and it was cheering to see the old bounty of nature gushing forth again in such unusual profusion and beauty, as if in pitiful charity for the troubles of mankind. I never saw the country look so rich in its spring robes as it does now.

CHAPTER III.

AMONG THE PRESTON OPERATIVES.

Proud Preston, or Priest-town, on the banks of the beautiful Ribble, is a place of many quaint customs, and of great historic fame. Its character for pride is said to come from the fact of its having been, in the old time, a favourite residence of the local nobles and gentry, and of many penniless folk with long pedigrees. It was here that Richard Arkwright shaved chins at a halfpenny each, in the meantime working out his bold and ingenious schemes, with patient faith in their ultimate success. It was here, too, that the teetotal movement first began, with Anderson for its rhyme-smith. Preston has had its full share of the changeful fortunes of England, and, like our motherland, it has risen strongly out of them all. War's mad havoc has swept over it in many a troubled period of our history. Plague, pestilence, and famine have afflicted it sorely; and it has suffered from trade riots, "plug-drawings," panics, and strikes of most disastrous kinds. Proud Preston--the town of the Stanleys and the Hoghtons, and of "many a crest that is famous in story"--the town where silly King Jamie disported himself a little, with his knights and nobles, during the time of his ruinous visit to Hoghton Tower,--Proud Preston has seen many a black day. But, from the time when Roman sentinels kept watch and ward in their old camp at Walton, down by the Ribble side, it has never seen so much wealth and so much bitter poverty together as now. The streets do not show this poverty; but it is there. Looking from Avenham Walks, that glorious landscape smiles in all the splendour of a rich spring-tide. In those walks the nursemaids and children, and dainty folk, are wandering as usual airing their curls in the fresh breeze; and only now and then a workless operative trails by with chastened look. The wail of sorrow is not heard in Preston market-place; but destitution may be found almost anywhere there just now, cowering in squalid corners, within a few yards of plenty--as I have seen it many a time this week. The courts and alleys behind even some of the main streets swarm with people who have hardly a whole nail left to scratch themselves with.

Before attempting to tell something of what I saw whilst wandering amongst the poor operatives of Preston, I will say at once, that I do not intend to meddle with statistics. They have been carefully gathered, and often given elsewhere, and there is no need for me to repeat them. But, apart from these, the theme is endless, and full of painful interest. I hear on all hands that there is hardly any town in Lancashire suffering so much as Preston. The reason why the stroke has fallen so heavily here, lies in the nature of the trade. In the first place, Preston is almost purely a cotton town. There are two or three flax mills, and two or three ironworks, of no great extent; but, upon the whole, there is hardly any variety of employment there to lighten the disaster which has befallen its one absorbing occupation. There is comparatively little weaving in Preston; it is a town mostly engaged in spinning. The cotton used there is nearly all what is called "Middling American," the very kind which is now most scarce and dear. The yarns of Preston are known by the name of "Blackburn Counts." They range from 28's up to 60's, and they enter largely into the manufacture of goods for the India market. These things partly explain why Preston is more deeply overshadowed by the particular gloom of the times than many other places in Lancashire. About half-past nine on Tuesday morning last, I set out with an old acquaintance to call upon a certain member of the Relief Committee, in George's Ward. He is the manager of a cotton mill in that quarter, and he is well known and much respected among the working people. When we entered the mill-yard, all was quiet there, and the factory was still and silent. But through the office window we could see the man we wanted. He was accompanied by one of the proprietors of the mill, turning over the relief books of the ward. I soon found that he had a strong sense of humour, as well as a heart welling over with tenderness. He pointed to some of the cases in his books. The first was that of an old man, an overlooker of a cotton mill. His family was thirteen in number; three of the children were under ten years of age; seven of the rest were factory operatives; but the whole family had been out of work for several months. When in full employment the joint earnings of the family amounted to 80s. a week; but, after struggling on in the hope of better times, and exhausting the savings of past labour, they had been brought down to the receipt of charity at last, and for sixteen weeks gone by the whole thirteen had been living upon 6s. a week from the relief fund. They had no other resource. I went to see them at their own house afterwards, and it certainly was a pattern of cleanliness, with the little household gods there still. Seeing that house, a stranger would never dream that the family was living on an average income of less than sixpence a head per week. But I know how hard some decent folk will struggle with the bitterest poverty before they will give in to it. The old man came in whilst I was there. He sat down in one corner, quietly tinkering away at something he had in his hands. His old corduroy trousers were well patched, and just new washed. He had very little to say to us, except that "He could like to get summat to do; for he wur tired o' walkin' abeawt." Another case was that of a poor widow woman, with five young children. This family had been driven from house to house, by increasing necessity, till they had sunk at last into a dingy little hovel, up a dark court, in one of the poorest parts of the town, where they huddled together about a fireless grate to keep one another warm. They had nothing left of the wreck of their home but two rickety chairs, and a little deal table reared against the wall, because one of the legs was gone. In this miserable hole--which I saw afterwards--her husband died of sheer starvation, as was declared by the jury on the inquest. The dark, damp hovel where they had crept to was scarcely four yards square; and the poor woman pointed to one corner of the floor, saying, "He dee'd i' that nook." He died there, with nothing to lie upon but the ground, and nothing to cover him, in that fireless hovel. His wife and children crept about him, there, to watch him die; and to keep him as warm as they could. When the relief committee first found this family out, the entire clothing of the family of seven persons weighed eight pounds, and sold for fivepence, as rags. I saw the family afterwards, at their poor place; and will say more about them hereafter. He told me of many other cases of a similar kind. But, after agreeing to a time when we should visit them personally, we set out together to see the "Stone Yard," where there are many factory hands at work under the Board of Guardians.

The "Stone Yard" is close by the Preston and Lancaster Canal. Here there are from one hundred and seventy to one hundred and eighty, principally young men, employed in breaking, weighing, and wheeling stone, for road mending. The stones are of a hard kind of blue boulder, gathered from the land between Kendal and Lancaster. The "Labour Master" told me that there were thousands of tons of these boulders upon the land between Kendal and Lancaster. A great deal of them are brought from a place called "Tewhitt Field," about seven mile on "t' other side o' Lancaster." At the "Stone Yard" it is all piece-work, and the men can come and go when they like. As one of the Guardians told me, "They can oather sit an' break 'em, or kneel an' break 'em, or lie deawn to it, iv they'n a mind." The men can choose whether they will fill three tons of the broken stone, and wheel it to the central heap, for a shilling, or break one ton for a shilling. The persons employed here are mostly "lads an' leet- timber't chaps." The stronger men are sent to work upon Preston Moor. There are great varieties of health and strength amongst them. "Beside," as the Labour Master said, "yo'd hardly believe what a difference there it i'th wark o' two men wortchin' at the same heap, sometimes. There's a great deal i'th breaker, neaw; some on 'em's more artful nor others. They finden out that they can break 'em as fast again at after they'n getten to th' wick i'th inside. I have known an' odd un or two, here, that could break four ton a day,--an' many that couldn't break one,--but then, yo' know, th' men can only do accordin' to their ability. There is these differences, and there always will be." As we stood talking together, one of my friends said that he wished "Radical Jack" had been there. The latter gentleman is one of the guardians of the poor, and superintendent of the "Stone Yard." The men are naturally jealous of misrepresentation; and, the other day, as "Radical Jack" was describing the working of the yard to a gentleman who had come to look at the scene, some of the men overheard his words, and, misconceiving their meaning, gathered around the superintendent, clamorously protesting against what he had been saying. "He's lying!" said one. "Look at these honds!" cried another; "Wi'n they ever be fit to go to th' factory wi' again?"

Others turned up the soles of their battered shoon, to show their cut and stockingless feet. They were pacified at last; but, after the superintendent had gone away, some of the men said much and more, and "if ever he towd ony moor lies abeawt 'em, they'd fling him into th' cut." The "Labour Master" told me there was a large wood shed for the men to shelter in when rain came on. As we were conversing, one of my friends exclaimed, "He's here now!" "Who's here?" "Radical Jack." The superintendent was coming down the road. He told me some interesting things, which I will return to on another occasion. But our time was up. We had other places to see. As we came away, three old Irishwomen leaned against the wall at the corner of the yard, watching the men at work inside. One of them was saying, "Thim guardians is the awfullest set o' min in the world! A man had better be transpoorted than come under 'em. An' thin, they'll try you, an' try you, as if you was goin' to be hanged." The poor old soul had evidently only a narrow view of the necessities and difficulties which beset the labours of the Board of Guardians at a time like this. On our way back to town one of my friends told me that he "had met a sexton the day before, and had asked him how trade was with him. The sexton replied that it was "Varra bad--nowt doin', hardly." "Well, how's that?" asked the other. "Well, thae sees," answered the sexton, "Poverty seldom dees. There's far more kilt wi' o'er-heytin' an' o'er-drinkin' nor there is wi' bein' pinched."

CHAPTER IV.

Leaving the "Stone Yard," to fulfil an engagement in another part of the town, we agreed to call upon three or four poor folk, who lived by the way; and I don't know that I could do better than say something about what I saw of them. As we walked along, one of my companions told me of an incident which happened to one of the visitors in another ward, a few days before. In the course of his round, this visitor called upon a certain destitute family which was under his care, and he found the husband sitting alone in the house, pale and silent. His wife had been "brought to bed" two or three days before; and the visitor inquired how she was getting on. "Hoo's very ill," said the husband. "And the child," continued the visitor, "how is it?" "It's deeod," replied the man; "it dee'd yesterday." He then rose, and walked slowly into the next room, returning with a basket in his hands, in which the dead child was decently laid out.

"That's o' that's laft on it neaw," said the poor fellow. Then, putting the basket upon the floor, he sat down in front of it, with his head between his hands, looking silently at the corpse. Such things as these were the theme of our conversation as we went along, and I found afterwards that every visitor whom it was my privilege to meet, had some special story of distress to relate, which came within his own appointed range of action. In my first flying visit to that great melancholy field, I could only glean such things as lay nearest to my hand, just then; but wherever I went, I heard and saw things which touchingly testify what noble stuff the working population of Lancashire, as a whole, is made of. One of the first cases we called upon, after leaving the "Stone Yard," was that of a family of ten--man and wife, and eight children. Four of the children were under ten years of age,--five were capable of working;

and, when the working part of the family was in full employment, their joint earnings amounted to 61s. per week. But, in this case, the mother's habitual ill-health had been a great expense in the household for several years. This family belonged to a class of operatives--a much larger class than people unacquainted with the factory districts are likely to suppose--a class of operatives which will struggle, in a dumb, enduring way, to the death, sometimes, before they will sacrifice that "immediate jewel of their souls"-- their old independence, and will keep up a decent appearance to the very last. These suffer more than the rest; for, in addition to the pains of bitter starvation, they feel a loss which is more afflicting to them even than the loss of food and furniture ; and their sufferings are less heard of than the rest, because they do not like to complain. This family of ten persons had been living, during the last nine weeks, upon relief amounting to 5s. a week. When we called, the mother and one or two of her daughters were busy in the next room, washing their poor bits of well-kept clothing. The daughters kept out of sight, as if ashamed. It was a good kind of cottage, in a clean street, called "Maudland Bank," and the whole place had a tidy, sweet look, though it was washing-day. The mother told me that she had been severely afflicted with seven successive attacks of inflammation, and yet, in spite of her long-continued ill-health, and in spite of the iron teeth of poverty which had been gnawing at them so long, for the first time, I have rarely seen a more frank and cheerful countenance than that thin matron's, as she stood there, wringing her clothes, and telling her little story. The house they lived in belonged to their late employer, whose mill stopped some time ago. We asked her how they managed to pay the rent, and she said, "Why, we dunnot pay it; we cannot pay it, an' he doesn't push us for it. Aw guess he knows he'll get it sometime. But we owe'd a deal o' brass beside that. Just look at this shop book. Aw'm noan freetend ov onybody seein' my acceawnts. An' then, there's a great lot o' doctor's-bills i' that pot, theer. Thoose are o' for me. There'll ha' to be some wark done afore things can be fotched up again. . . . Eh; aw'll tell yo what, William, (this was addressed to the visitor,) it went ill again th' grain wi' my husband to goo afore th' Board. An' when he did goo, he wouldn't say so mich. Yo known, folk doesn't like brastin' off abeawt theirsel' o' at once, at a shop like that. . . . Aw think sometimes it's very weel that four ov eawrs are i' heaven,--we'n sich hard tewin' (toiling), to poo through wi' tother, just neaw. But, aw guess it'll not last for ever." As we came away, talking of the reluctance shown by the better sort of working people to ask for relief, or even sometimes to accept it when offered to them, until thoroughly starved to it, I was told of a visitor calling upon a poor woman in another ward; no application had been made for relief, but some kind neighbour had told the committee that the woman and her husband were "ill off." The visitor, finding that they were perishing for want, offered the woman some relief tickets for food; but the poor soul began to cry, and said; "Eh, aw dar not touch 'em; my husban' would sauce me so! Aw dar not take 'em; aw should never yer the last on't!" When we got to the lower end of Hope Street, my guide stopped suddenly, and said, "Oh, this is close to where that woman lives whose husband died of starvation. "Leading a few yards up the by-street, he turned into a low, narrow entry, very dark and damp. Two turns more brought us to a dirty, pent-up corner, where a low door stood open. We entered there. It was a cold, gloomy-looking little hovel. In my allusion to the place last week I said it was "scarcely four yards square." It is not more than three yards square. There was no fire in the little rusty grate. The day was sunny, but no sunshine could ever reach that nook, nor any fresh breezes disturb the pestilent vapours that harboured there, festering in the sluggish gloom. In one corner of the place a little worn and broken stair led up to a room of the same size above, where, I was told, there was now some straw for the family to sleep upon. But the only furniture in the house, of any kind, was two rickety chairs and a little broken deal table, reared against the stairs, because one leg was gone. A quiet-looking, thin woman, seemingly about fifty years of age, sat there, when we went in. She told us that she had buried five of her children, and that she had six yet alive, all living with her in that poor place. They had no work, no income whatever, save what came from the Relief Committee. Five of the children were playing in and out, bare-footed, and, like the mother, miserably clad; but they seemed quite unconscious that anything ailed them. I never saw finer children anywhere. The eldest girl, about fourteen, came in whilst we were there, and she leaned herself bashfully against the wall for a minute or two, and then slunk slyly out again, as if ashamed of our presence. The poor widow pointed to the cold corner where her husband died lately. She said that "his name was Tim Pedder. His fadder name was Timothy, an' his mudder name was Mary. He was a driver (a driver of boat-horses on the canal); but he had bin oot o' work a lang time afore he dee'd." I found in this case, as in some others, that the poor body had not much to say about her distress; but she did not need to say much. My guide told me that when he first called upon the family, in the depth of last winter, he found the children all clinging round about their mother in the cold hovel, trying in that way to keep one another warm. The time for my next appointment was now hard on, and we hurried towards the shop in Fishergate, kept by the gentleman I had promised to meet. He is an active member of the Relief Committee, and a visitor in George's ward. We found him in. He had just returned from the "Cheese Fair," at Lancaster. My purpose was to find out what time on the morrow we could go together to see some of the cases he was best acquainted with. But, as the evening was not far spent, he proposed that we should go at once to see a few of those which were nearest. We set out together to Walker's Court, in Friargate. The first place we entered was at the top of the little narrow court. There we found a good-tempered Irish-woman sitting without fire, in her feverish hovel. "Well, missis," said the visitor, "how is your husband getting on?" "Ah, well, now, Mr. T----," replied she, "you know, he's only a delicate little man, an' a tailor; an' he wint to work on the moor, an' he couldn't stand it. Sure, it was draggin' the bare life out of him. So, he says to me, one morning, "Catharine," says he, "I'll lave off this a little while, till I see will I be able to get a job o' work at my own trade; an' maybe God will rise up some thin' to put a dud o' clothes on us all, an' help us to pull through till the black time is over us." So, I told him to try his luck, any way; for he was killin' himself entirely on the moor. An' so he did try; for there's not an idle bone in that same boy's skin. But, see this, now; there's nothin' in the world to be had to do just now-- an' a dale too many waitin' to do it--so all he got by the change was losin' his work on the moor. There is himself, an' me, an' the seven childer. Five o' the childer is under tin year old. We are all naked; an' the house is bare; an' our health is gone wi' the want o' mate. Sure it wasn't in the likes o' this we wor livin' when times was good." Three of the youngest children were playing about on the floor. "That's a very fine lad," said I, pointing to one of them. The little fellow blushed, and smiled, and then became very still and attentive. "Ah, thin," said his mother, "that villain's the boy for tuckin' up soup! The Lord be about him, an' save him alive to me,--the crayter ! . . . An' there's little curly there,-- the rogue! Sure he'll take as much soup as any wan o' them. Maybe he wouldn't laugh to see a big bowl forninst him this day." "It's very well they have such good spirits," said the visitor. "So it is," replies the woman, "so it is, for God knows it's little else they have to keep them warm thim bad times."

CHAPTER V.

The next house we called at in Walker's Court was much like the first in appearance--very little left but the walls, and that little, such as none but the neediest would pick up, if it was thrown out to the streets. The only person in the place was a pale, crippled woman; her sick head, lapped in a poor white clout, swayed languidly to and fro. Besides being a cripple, she had been ill six years, and now her husband, also, was taken ill. He had just crept off to fetch medicine for the two. We did not stop here long. The hand of the Ancient Master was visible in that pallid face; those sunken eyes, so full of deathly langour, seemed to be wandering about in dim, flickering gazes, upon the confines of an unknown world. I think that woman will soon be "where the weary are at rest." As we came out, she said, slowly, and in broken, painful utterances, that "she hoped the Lord would open the heavens for those who had helped them." A little lower down the court, we peeped in at two other doorways. The people were well known to my companion, who has the charge of visiting this part of the ward. Leaning against the door-cheek of one of these dim, unwholesome hovels, he said, "Well, missis; how are you getting on?" There was a tall, thin woman inside. She seemed to be far gone in some exhausting illness. With slow difficulty she rose to her feet, and, setting her hands to her sides, gasped out, "My coals are done." He made a note, and said, I'll send you some more." Her other wants were regularly seen to on a certain day every week. Ours was an accidental visit. We now turned up to another nook of the court, where my companion told me there was a very bad case. He found the door fast. We looked through the window into that miserable man-nest. It was cold, gloomy, and bare. As Corrigan says, in the "Colleen Bawn," "There was nobody in--but the fire--and that was gone out." As we came away, a stalwart Irishman met us at a turn of the court, and said to my companion, "Sure, ye didn't visit this house." " Not to-day;" replied the visitor. "I'll come and see you at the usual time." The people in this house were not so badly off as some others. We came down the steps of the court into the fresher air of Friargate again.

Our next walk was to Heatley Street. As we passed by a cluster of starved loungers, we overheard one of them saying to another, "Sitho, yon's th' soup-maister, gooin' a-seein' somebry." Our time was getting short, so we only called at one house in Heatley Street, where there was a family of eleven--a decent family, a well-kept and orderly household, though now stript almost to the bare ground of all worldly possession, sold, bitterly, piecemeal, to help to keep the bare life together, as sweetly as possible, till better days. The eldest son is twenty-seven years of age. The whole family has been out of work for the last seventeen weeks, and before that, they had been working only short time for seven months. For thirteen weeks they had lived upon less than one shilling a head per week, and I am not sure that they did not pay the rent out of that; and now the income of the whole eleven is under 16s., with rent to pay. In this house they hold weekly prayer-meetings. Thin picking--one shilling a week, or less--for all expenses, for one person. It is easier to write about it than to feel what it means, unless one has tried it for three or four months. Just round the corner from Heatley Street, we stopped at the open door of a very little cottage. A good-looking young Irishwoman sat there, upon a three- legged stool, suckling her child. She was clean; and had an intelligent look. "Let's see, missis," said the visitor, "what do you pay for this nook?" "We pay eighteenpence a week--and they WILL have it--my word." "Well, an' what income have you now?" "We have eighteenpence a head in the week, an' the rent to pay out o' that, or else they'll turn us out." Of course, the visitor knew that this was true; but he wanted me to hear the people speak for themselves. "Let's see, Missis Burns, your husband's name is Patrick, isn't it?" " Yes, sir; Patrick Burns." "What! Patrick Burns, the famous foot- racer?" The little woman smiled bashfully, and replied, "Yes, sir; I suppose it is." With respect to what the woman said about having to pay her rent or turn out, I may remark, in passing, that I have not hitherto met with an instance in which any millowner, or wealthy man, having cottage property, has pressed the unemployed poor for rent. But it is well to remember that there is a great amount of cottage property in Preston, as in other manufacturing towns, which belongs to the more provident class of working men. These working men, now hard pressed by the general distress, have been compelled to fall back upon their little rentals, clinging to them as their last independent means of existence. They are compelled to this, for, if they cannot get work, they cannot get anything else, having property. These are becoming fewer, however, from day to day. The poorest are hanging a good deal upon those a little less poor than themselves; and every link in the lengthening chain of neediness is helping to pull down the one immediately above it. There is, also, a considerable amount of cottage property in Preston, belonging to building societies, which have enough to do to hold their own just now. And then there is always some cottage property in the hands of agents.

Leaving Heatley Street, we went to a place called "Seed's Yard." Here we called upon a clean old stately widow, with a calm, sad face. She had been long known, and highly respected, in a good street, not far off, where she had lived for twenty-four years, in fair circumstances, until lately. She had always owned a good houseful of furniture; but, after making bitter meals upon the gradual wreck of it, she had been compelled to break up that house, and retire with her five children to lodge with a lone widow in this little cot, not over three yards square, in "Seed's Yard," one of those dark corners into which decent poverty is so often found now, creeping unwillingly away from the public eye, in the hope of weathering the storm of adversity, in penurious independence. The old woman never would accept relief from the parish, although the whole family had been out of work for many months. One of the daughters, a clean, intelligent-looking young woman, about eighteen, sat at the table, eating a little bread and treacle to a cup of light-coloured tea, when we went in; but she blushed, and left off until we had gone--which was not long after. It felt almost like sacrilege to peer thus into the privacies of such people; but I hope they did not feel as if it had been done offensively. We called next at the cottage of a hand-loom weaver--a poor trade now in the best of times--a very poor trade--since the days when tattered old "Jem Ceawp" sung his pathetic song of "Jone o' Greenfeelt"--

"Aw'm a poor cotton weighver, as ony one knows; We'n no meight i'th heawse, an' we'n worn eawt er clothes; We'n live't upo nettles, while nettles were good; An' Wayterloo porritch is th' most of er food; This clemmin' and starvin', Wi' never a farthin'-- It's enough to drive ony mon mad."

This family was four in number--man, wife, and two children. They had always lived near to the ground, for the husband's earnings at the loom were seldom more than 7s. for a full week. The wife told us that they were not receiving any relief, for she said that when her husband "had bin eawt o' wark a good while he turn't his hond to shaving;" and in this way the ingenious struggling fellow had scraped a thin living for them during many months. "But," said she, " it brings varra little in, we hev to trust so much. He shaves four on 'em for a haw-penny, an' there's a deal on 'em connot pay that. Yo know, they're badly off--(the woman seemed to think her circumstances rather above the common kind);

an' then," continued she, "when they'n run up a shot for three-hawpence or twopence or so, they cannot pay it o' no shap, an' so they stoppen away fro th' shop. They cannot for shame come, that's heaw it is; so we lose'n their custom till sich times as summat turns up at they can raise a trifle to pay up wi'. . . . He has nobbut one razzor, but it'll be like to do." Hearken this, oh, ye spruce Figaros of the city, who trim the clean, crisp whiskers of the well-to-do! Hearken this, ye dainty perruquiers, "who look so brisk, and smell so sweet," and have such an exquisite knack of chirruping, and lisping, and sliding over the smooth edge of the under lip,--and, sometimes, agreeably too,--"an infinite deal of nothing,"--ye who clip and anoint the hair of Old England's curled darlings! Eight chins a penny; and three months' credit! A bodle a piece for mowing chins overgrown with hair like pin-wire, and thick with dust; how would you like that? How would you get through it all, with a family of four, and only one razor? The next place we called at was what my friend described, in words that sounded to me, somehow, like melancholy irony,--as "a poor provision shop." It was, indeed, a poor shop for provender. In the window, it is true, there were four or five empty glasses, where children's spice had once been. There was a little deal shelf here and there; but there were neither sand, salt, whitening, nor pipes. There was not the ghost of a farthing candle, nor a herring, nor a marble, nor a match, nor of any other thing, sour or sweet, eatable or saleable for other uses, except one small mug full of buttermilk up in a corner--the last relic of a departed trade, like the "one rose of the wilderness, left on its stalk to mark where a garden has been." But I will say more about this in the next chapter.

CHAPTER VI.

Returning to the little shop mentioned in my last--the "little provision shop," where there was nothing left to eat--nothing, indeed, of any kind, except one mug of buttermilk, and a miserable remnant of little empty things, which nobody would buy; four or five glass bottles in the window, two or three poor deal shelves, and a doleful little counter, rudely put together, and looking as if it felt, now, that there was nothing in the world left for it but to become chips at no distant date. Everything in the place had a sad, subdued look, and seemed conscious of having come down in the world, without hope of ever rising again; even the stript walls appeared to look at one another with a stony gaze of settled despair. But there was a clean, matronly woman in the place, gliding about from side to side with a cloth in her hands, and wiping first one, then another, of these poor little relics of better days in a caressing way. The shop had been her special care when times were good, and she clung affectionately to its ruins still. Besides, going about cleaning and arranging the little empty things in this way looked almost like doing business. But, nevertheless, the woman had a cheerful, good-humoured countenance. The sunshine of hope was still warm in her heart; though there was a touch of pathos in the way she gave the little rough counter another kindly wipe now and then, as if she wished to keep its spirits up; and in the way she looked, now at the buttermilk mug, then at the open door, and then at the four glass bottles in the window, which had been gazed at so oft and so eagerly by little children outside, in the days when spice was in them. . . . The husband came in from the little back room. He was a hardy, frank-looking man, and, like his wife, a trifle past middle age, I thought; but he had nothing to say, as he stood there with his wife, by the counter side. She answered our questions freely and simply, and in an uncomplaining way, not making any attempt to awaken sympathy by enlarging upon the facts of their condition. Theirs was a family of seven--man, wife, and five children. The man was a spinner; and his thrifty wife had managed the little shop, whilst he worked at the mill. There are many striving people among the factory operatives, who help up the family earnings by keeping a little shop in this way. But this family was another of those instances in which working people have been pulled down by misfortune before the present crisis came on. Just previous to the mills beginning to work short time, four of their five children had been lying ill, all at once, for five months; and, before that trouble befell them, one of the lads had two of his fingers taken off, whilst working at the factory, and so was disabled a good while. It takes little additional weight to sink those whose chins are only just above water; and these untoward circumstances oiled the way of this struggling family to the ground, before the mills stopped. A few months' want of work, with their little stock of shop stuff oozing away--partly on credit to their poor neighbours, and partly to live upon themselves --and they become destitute of all, except a few beggarly remnants of empty shop furniture. Looking round the place, I said," Well, missis, how's trade?" "Oh, brisk," said she; and then the man and his wife smiled at one another. "Well," said I, "yo'n sowd up, I see, heawever." "Ay," answered she, "we'n sowd up, for sure--a good while sin';" and then she smiled again, as if she thought she had said a clever thing. They had been receiving relief from the parish several weeks; but she told me that some ill-natured neighbour had "set it eawt," that they had sold off their stock out of the shop, and put the money into the bank. Through this report, the Board of Guardians had "knocked off" their relief for a fortnight, until the falsity of the report was made clear. After that, the Board gave orders for the man and his wife and three of the children to be admitted to the workhouse, leaving the other two lads, who were working at the "Stone Yard," to "fend for theirsels," and find new nests wherever they could. This, however, was overruled afterwards; and the family is still holding together in the empty shop,--receiving from all sources, work and relief, about 13s. a week for the seven,--not bad, compared with the income of very many others. It is sad to think how many poor families get sundered and scattered about the world in a time like this, never to meet again. And the false report respecting this family in the little shop, reminds me that the poor are not always kind to the poor. I learnt, from a gentleman who is Secretary to the Relief Committee of one of the wards, that it is not uncommon for the committees to receive anonymous letters, saying that so and so is unworthy of relief, on some ground or other. These complaints were generally found to be either wholly false, or founded upon some mistake. I have three such letters now before me. The first, written on a torn scrap of ruled paper, runs thus:--"May 19th, 1862.--If you please be so kind as to look after __ Back Newton Street Formerly a Resident of __ as i think he is not Deserving Relief.--A Ratepayer." In each case I give the spelling, and everything else, exactly as in the originals before me, except the names. The next of these epistles says:-- "Preston, May 29th.--Sir, I beg to inform you that __, of Park Road, in receipt from the Relief Fund, is a very unworthy person, having worked two days since the 16 and drunk the remainder and his wife also; for the most part, he has plenty of work for himself his wife and a journeyman but that is their regular course of life. And the S___s have all their family working full time. Yours respectfully." These last two are anonymous. The next is written in a very good hand, upon a square piece of very blue writing paper. It has a name attached, but no address:--"Preston, June 2nd, 1862.--Mr. Dunn,-- Dear Sir, Would you please to inquire into the case of __, of __. the are a family of 3 the man work four or more days per week on the moor the woman works 6 days per week at Messrs Simpsons North Road the third is a daughter 13 or 14 should be a weaver but to lasey she has good places such as Mr. Hollins and Horrocks and Millers as been sent a way for being to lasey. the man and woman very fond of drink. I as a Nabour and a subscriber do not think this a proper case for your charity. Yours truly, __." The committee could not find out the writer of this, although a name is given. Such things as these need no comment.

The next house we called at was inhabited by an old widow and her only daughter. The daughter had been grievously afflicted with disease of the heart, and quite incapable of helping herself during the last eleven years. The poor worn girl sat upon an old tattered kind of sofa, near the fire, panting for breath in the close atmosphere. She sat there in feverish helplessness, sallow and shrunken, and unable to bear up her head. It was a painful thing to look at her. She had great difficulty in uttering a few words. I can hardly guess what her age may be now; I should think about twenty-five. Mr Toulmin, one of the visitors who accompanied me to the place, reminded the young woman of his having called upon them there more than four years ago, to leave some bedding which had been bestowed upon an old woman by a certain charity in the town. He saw no more of them after that, until the present hard times began, when he was deputed by the Relief Committee to call at that distressed corner amongst others in his own neighbourhood; and when he first opened the door, after a lapse of four years, he was surprised to find the same young woman, sitting in the same place, gasping painfully for breath, as he had last seen her. The old widow had just been able to earn what kept soul and body together in her sick girl and herself, during the last eleven years, by washing and such like work. But even this resource had fallen away a good deal during these bad times; there are so many poor creatures like herself, driven to extremity, and glad to grasp at any little bit of employment which can be had. In addition to what the old woman could get by a day's washing now and then, she received 1s. 6d. a week from the parish. Think of the poor old soul trailing about the world, trying to "scratch a living" for herself and her daughter by washing; and having to hurry home from her labour to attend to that sick girl through eleven long years. Such a life is a good deal like a slow funeral. It is struggling for a few breaths more, with the worms crawling over you. And yet I am told that the old woman was not accustomed to "make a poor mouth," as the saying goes. How true it is that "a great many people in this world have only one form of rhetoric for their profoundest experiences, namely--to waste away and die."

Our next visit was to an Irish family. There was an old woman in, and a flaxen-headed lad about ten years of age. She was sitting upon a low chair,--the only seat in the place,--and the tattered lad was kneeling on the ground before her, whilst she combed his hair out. "Well, missis, how are you getting on amongst it?" "Oh, well, then, just middlin', Mr T. Ye see, I am busy combin' this boy's hair a bit, for 'tis gettin' like a wisp o' hay." There was not a vestige of furniture in the cottage, except the chair the old woman sat on. She said, "I did sell the childer's bedstead for 2s. 6d.; an' after that I sold the bed from under them for 1s. 6d., just to keep them from starvin' to death. The childer had been two days without mate then, an' faith I couldn't bear it any longer. After that I did sell the big pan, an' then the new rockin' chair, an' so on, one thing after another, till all wint entirely, barrin' this I am sittin' on, an' they wint for next to nothin' too. Sure, I paid 9s. 6d. for the bed itself, which was sold for 1s. 6d. We all sleep on straw now." This family was seven in number. The mill at which they used to work had been stopped about ten months. One of the family had found employment at another mill, three months out of the ten, and the old man himself had got a few days' work in that time. The rest of the family had been wholly unemployed, during the ten months. Except the little money this work brought in, and a trifle raised now and then by the sale of a bit of furniture when hunger and cold pressed them hard, the whole family had been living upon 5s. a week for the last ten months. The rent was running on. The eldest daughter was twenty- eight years of age. As we came away Mr Toulmin said to me, "Well, I have called at that house regularly for the last sixteen weeks, and this is the first time I ever saw a fire in the place. But the old man has got two days' work this week--that may account for the fire."

It was now close upon half-past seven in the evening, at which time I had promised to call upon the Secretary of the Trinity Ward Relief Committee, whose admirable letter in the London Times, attracted so much attention about a month ago. I met several members of the committee at his lodgings, and we had an hour's interesting conversation. I learnt that, in cases of sickness arising from mere weakness, from poorness of diet, or from unsuitableness of the food commonly provided by the committee, orders were now issued for such kind of "kitchen physic" as was recommended by the doctors. The committee had many cases of this kind. One instance was mentioned, in which, by the doctor's advice, four ounces of mutton chop daily had been ordered to be given to a certain sick man, until further notice. The thing went on and was forgotten, until one day, when the distributor of food said to the committeeman who had issued the order, "I suppose I must continue that daily mutton chop to so-and- so?" "Eh, no; he's been quite well two months?" The chop had been going on for ninety-five days. We had some talk with that class of operatives who are both clean, provident, and "heawse-preawd," as Lancashire folk call it. The Secretary told me that he was averse to such people living upon the sale of their furniture; and the committee had generally relieved the distress of such people, just as if they had no furniture, at all. He mentioned the case of a family of factory operatives, who were all fervent lovers of music, as so many of the working people of Lancashire are. Whilst in full work, they had scraped up money to buy a piano; and, long after the ploughshare of ruin had begun to drive over the little household, they clung to the darling instrument, which was such a source of pure pleasure to them, and they were advised to keep it by the committee which relieved them. "Yes," said another member of the committee," but I called there lately, and the piano's gone at last." Many interesting things came out in the course of our conversation. One mentioned a house he had called at, where there was neither chair, table, nor bed; and one of the little lads had to hold up a piece of board for him to write upon. Another spoke of the difficulties which "lone women" have to encounter in these hard times. "I knocked so-and-so off my list," said one of the committee, "till I had inquired into an ill report I heard of her. But she came crying to me; and I found out that the woman had been grossly belied." Another (Mr Nowell) told of a house on his list, where they had no less than one hundred and fifty pawn tickets. He told, also, of a moulder's family, who had been all out of work and starving so long, that their poor neighbours came at last and recommended the committee to relieve them, as they would not apply for relief themselves. They accepted relief just one week, and then the man came and said that he had a PROSPECT of work; and he shouldn't need relief tickets any longer. It was here that I heard so much about anonymous letters, of which I have given you three samples. Having said that I should like to see the soup kitchen, one of the committee offered to go with me thither at six o'clock the next morning; and so I came away from the meeting in the cool twilight.

Old Preston looked fine to me in the clear air of that declining day. I stood a while at the end of the "Bull" gateway. There was a comical-looking little knock-kneed fellow in the middle of the street --a wandering minstrel, well known in Preston by the name of "Whistling Jack." There he stood, warbling and waving his band, and looking from side to side,--in vain. At last I got him to whistle the "Flowers of Edinburgh." He did it, vigorously; and earned his penny well. But even "Whistling Jack" complained of the times. He said Preston folk had "no taste for music." But he assured me the time would come when there would be a monument to him in that town.

CHAPTER VII.

About half-past six I found my friend waiting at the end of the "Bull" gateway. It was a lovely morning. The air was cool and clear, and the sky was bright. It was easy to see which was the way to the soup kitchen, by the stragglers going and coming. We passed the famous "Orchard," now a kind of fairground, which has been the scene of so many popular excitements in troubled times. All was quiet in the "Orchard" that morning, except that, here, a starved-looking woman, with a bit of old shawl tucked round her head, and a pitcher in her hand, and there, a bare-footed lass, carrying a tin can, hurried across the sunny space towards the soup kitchen. We passed a new inn, called "The Port Admiral." On the top of the building there were three life-sized statues--Wellington and Nelson, with the Greek slave between them--a curious companionship. These statues reminded me of a certain Englishman riding through Dublin, for the first time, upon an Irish car. "What are the three figures yonder?" said he to the car-boy, pointing to the top of some public building. "Thim three is the twelve apostles, your honour," answered the driver. "Nay, nay," said the traveller,"that'll not do. How do you make twelve out of three?" "Bedad," replied the driver, "your honour couldn't expect the whole twelve to be out at once such a murtherin' wet day as this." But we had other things than these to think of that day. As we drew near the baths and washhouses, where the soup kitchen is, the stream of people increased. About the gate there was a cluster of melancholy loungers, looking cold and hungry. They were neither going in nor going away. I was told afterwards that many of these were people who had neither money nor tickets for food--some of them wanderers from town to town; anybody may meet them limping, footsore and forlorn, upon the roads in Lancashire, just now-- houseless wanderers, who had made their way to the soup kitchen to beg a mouthful from those who were themselves at death's door. In the best of times there are such wanderers; and, in spite of the generous provision made for the relief of the poor, there must be, in a time like the present, a great number who let go their hold of home (if they have any), and drift away in search of better fortune, and, sometimes, into irregular courses of life, never to settle more. Entering the yard, we found the wooden sheds crowded with people at breakfast--all ages, from white-haired men, bent with years, to eager childhood, yammering over its morning meal, and careless till the next nip of hunger came. Here and there a bonny lass had crept into the shade with her basin; and there was many a brown-faced man, who had been hardened by working upon the moor or at the "stone-yard." "Theer, thae's shap't that at last, as how?" said one of these to his friend, who had just finished and stood wiping his mouth complacently. "Shap't that," replied the other, "ay, lad, aw can do a ticket and a hafe (three pints of soup) every morning." Five hundred people breakfast in the sheds alone, every day. The soup kitchen opens at five in the morning, and there is always a crowd waiting to get in. This looks like the eagerness of hunger. I was told that they often deliver 3000 quarts of soup at this kitchen in two hours. The superintendent of the bread department informed me that, on that morning, he had served out two thousand loaves, of 3lb. 11oz. each. There was a window at one end, where soup was delivered to such as brought money for it instead of tickets. Those who came with tickets--by far the greatest number-- had to pass in single file through a strong wooden maze, which restrained their eagerness, and compelled them to order. I noticed that only a small proportion of men went through the maze; they were mostly women and children. There was many a fine, intelligent young face hurried blushing through that maze--many a bonny lad and lass who will be heard of honourably hereafter. The variety of utensils presented showed that some of the poor souls had been hard put to it for things to fetch their soup in. One brought a pitcher; another a bowl; and another a tin can, a world too big for what it had to hold. "Yo mun mind th' jug," said one old woman; "it's cracked, an' it's noan o' mine." "Will ye bring me some?" said a little, light- haired lass, holding up her rosy neb to the soupmaster. "Aw want a ha'poth," said a lad with a three-quart can in his hand. The benevolent-looking old gentleman who had taken the superintendence of the soup department as a labour of love, told me that there had been a woman there by half-past five that morning, who had come four miles for some coffee. There was a poor fellow breakfasting in the shed at the same time; and he gave the woman a thick shive of his bread as she went away. He mentioned other instances of the same humane feeling; and he said, "After what I have seen of them here, I say, 'Let me fall into the hands of the poor.'"

"They who, half-fed, feed the breadless, in the travail of distress; They who, taking from a little, give to those who still have less; They who, needy, yet can pity when they look on greater need; These are Charity's disciples,--these are Mercy's sons indeed."

We returned to the middle of the town just as the shopkeepers in Friargate were beginning to take their shutters down. I had another engagement at half-past nine. A member of the Trinity Ward Relief Committee, who is master of the Catholic school in that ward, had offered to go with me to visit some distressed people who were under his care in that part of the town. We left Friargate at the appointed time. As we came along there was a crowd in front of Messrs Wards', the fishmongers. A fine sturgeon had just been brought in. It had been caught in the Ribble that morning. We went in to look at the royal fish. It was six feet long, and weighed above a hundred pounds. I don't know that I ever saw a sturgeon before. But we had other fish to fry; and so we went on. The first place we called at was a cellar in Nile Street. "Here," said my companion, "let us have a look at old John." A gray-headed little man, of seventy, lived down in this one room, sunken from the street. He had been married forty years, and if I remember aright, he lost his wife about four years ago. Since that time, he had lived in this cellar, all alone, washing and cooking for himself. But I think the last would not trouble him much, for "they have no need for fine cooks who have only one potato to their dinner." When a lad, he had been apprenticed to a bobbin turner. Afterwards he picked up some knowledge of engineering; and he had been "well off in his day." He now got a few coppers occasionally from the poor folk about, by grinding knives, and doing little tinkering jobs. Under the window he had a rude bench, with a few rusty tools upon it, and in one corner there was a low, miserable bedstead, without clothing upon it. There was one cratchinly chair in the place, too; but hardly anything else. He had no fire; be generally went into neighbours' houses to warm himself. He was not short of such food as the Relief Committees bestow. There was a piece of bread upon the bench, left from his morning meal; and the old fellow chirruped about, and looked as blithe as if he was up to the middle in clover. He showed us a little thing which he had done "for a bit ov a prank." The number of his cellar was 8, and he had cut out a large tin figure of 8, a foot long, and nailed it upon his door, for the benefit of some of his friends that were getting bad in their eyesight, and "couldn't read smo' print so low deawn as that." "Well, John," said my companion, when we went in, "how are you getting on?" "Oh, bravely," replied he, handing a piece of blue paper to the inquirer, "bravely; look at that!" Why, this is a summons," said my companion. "Ay, bigad is't, too," answered the old man. "Never had sich a thing i' my life afore! Think o' me gettin' a summons for breakin' windows at seventy year owd. A bonny warlock, that, isn't it? Why, th' whole street went afore th' magistrates to get mo off." "Then you did get off, John?" "Get off! Sure, aw did. It wur noan o' me. It wur a keaw jobber, at did it. . . . Aw'll tell yo what, for two pins aw'd frame that summons, an' hang it eawt o' th' window; but it would look so impudent." Old John's wants were inquired into, and we left him fiddling among his rusty tools. We next went to a place called Hammond's Row--thirteen poor cottages, side by side. Twelve of the thirteen were inhabited by people living, almost entirely, upon relief, either from the parish or from the Relief Committee. There was only one house where no relief was needed. As we passed by, the doors were nearly all open, and the interiors all presented the same monotonous phase of destitution. They looked as if they had been sacked by bum-bailiffs. The topmost house was the only place where I saw a fire. A family of eight lived there. They were Irish people. The wife, a tall, cheerful woman, sat suckling her child, and giving a helping hand now and then to her husband's work. He was a little, pale fellow, with only one arm, and he had an impediment in his speech. He had taken to making cheap boxes of thin, rough deal, afterwards covered with paper. With the help of his wife he could make one in a day, and he got ninepence profit out of it--when the box was sold. He was working at one when we went in, and he twirled it proudly about with his one arm, and stammered out a long explanation about the way it had been made; and then he got upon the lid, and sprang about a little, to let us see how much it would bear. As the brave little tattered man stood there upon the box-lid, springing, and sputtering, and waving his one arm, his wife looked up at him with a smile, as if she thought him "the greatest wight on ground." There was a little curly-headed child standing by, quietly taking in all that was going on. I laid my hand upon her head; and asked her what her name was. She popped her thumb into her mouth, and looked shyly about from one to another, but never a word could I get her to say. "That's Lizzy," said the woman; "she is a little visitor belongin' to one o' the neighbours. They are badly off, and she often comes in. Sure, our childer is very fond of her, an' so she is of them. She is fine company wid ourselves, but always very shy wid strangers. Come now, Lizzy, darlin'; tell us your name, love, won't you, now?" But it was no use; we couldn't get her to speak. In the next cottage where we called, in this row, there was a woman washing. Her mug was standing upon a stool in the middle of the floor; and there was not any other thing in the place in the shape of furniture or household utensil. The walls were bare of everything, except a printed paper, bearing these words:

"The wages of sin is death. But the gift of God is eternal life, through Jesus Christ our Lord." We now went to another street, and visited the cottage of a blind chairmaker, called John Singleton. He was a kind of oracle among the poor folk of the neighbourhood. The old chairmaker was sitting by the fire when we went in; and opposite to him sat "Old John," the hero of the broken windows in Nile Street. He had come up to have a crack with his blind crony. The chairmaker was seventy years of age, and he had benefited by the advantage of good fundamental instruction in his youth. He was very communicative. He said he should have been educated for the priesthood, at Stonyhurst College. "My clothes were made, an' everything was ready for me to start to Stonyhurst. There was a stagecoach load of us going; but I failed th' heart, an' wouldn't go--an' I've forethought ever sin'. Mr Newby said to my friends at the same time, he said, 'You don't need to be frightened of him; he'll make the brightest priest of all the lot--an' I should, too. . . . I consider mysel' a young man yet, i' everything, except it be somethin' at's uncuth to me."

And now, old John, the grinder, began to complain again of how badly he had been used about the broken windows in Nile Street. But the old chairmaker stopped him; and, turning up his blind eyes, he said, "John, don't you be foolish. Bother no moor abeawt it. All things has but a time."

CHAPTER VIII.

A man cannot go wrong in Trinity Ward just now, if he wants to see poor folk. He may find them there at any time, but now he cannot help but meet them; and nobody can imagine how badly off they are, unless he goes amongst them. They are biding the hard time out wonderfully well, and they will do so to the end. They certainly have not more than a common share of human frailty. There are those who seem to think that when people are suddenly reduced to poverty, they should become suddenly endowed with the rarest virtues; but it never was so, and, perhaps, never will be so long as the world rolls. In my rambles about this ward, I was astonished at the dismal succession of destitute homes, and the number of struggling owners of little shops, who were watching their stocks sink gradually down to nothing, and looking despondingly at the cold approach of pauperism. I was astonished at the strings of dwellings, side by side, stript, more or less, of the commonest household utensils--the poor little bare houses, often crowded with lodgers, whose homes had been broken up elsewhere; sometimes crowded, three or four families of decent working people in a cottage of half-a-crown a-week rental; sleeping anywhere, on benches or on straw, and afraid to doff their clothes at night time because they had no other covering. Now and then the weekly visitor comes to the door of a house where he has regularly called. He lifts the latch, and finds the door locked. He looks in at the window. The house is empty, and the people are gone- -the Lord knows where. Who can tell what tales of sorrow will have their rise in the pressure of a time like this--tales that will never be written, and that no statistics will reveal.

Trinity Ward swarms with factory operatives; and, after our chat with blind John, the chairmaker, and his ancient crony the grinder from Nile Street, we set off again to see something more of them. Fitful showers came down through the day, and we had to shelter now and then. In one cottage, where we stopped a few minutes, the old woman told us that, in addition to their own family, they had three young women living with them--the orphan daughters of her husband's brother. They had been out of work thirty-four weeks, and their uncle--a very poor man--had been obliged to take them into his house, "till sich times as they could afford to pay for lodgin's somewheer else." My companion asked whether they were all out of work still. "Naw," replied the old woman, "one on 'em has getten on to wortch a few days for t' sick (that is, in the place of some sick person). Hoo's wortchin' i' th' cardreawn at 'Th' Big-un.'" (This is the name they give to Messrs Swainson and Birley's mill.)

The next place we called at was the house of an old joiner. He was lying very ill upstairs. As we drew up to the door, my companion said, "Now, this is a clean, respectable family. They have struggled hard and suffered a great deal, before they would ask for relief." When we went in, the wife was cleaning her well-nigh empty house. "Eh," said she," I thought it wur th' clubman comin', an' I wur just goin' to tell him that I had nothin' for him." The family was seven in number--man, wife, and five children. The husband, as I have said, was lying ill. The wife told me that they had only 6s. a-week coming in for the seven to live upon. My companion was the weekly visitor who relieved them. She told me that her husband was sixty- eight years old; she was not forty. She said that her husband was not strong, and he had been going nearly barefoot and "clemmed" all through last winter, and she was afraid he had got his death of cold. They had not a bed left to lie upon. "My husband," said she,"was a master joiner once, an' was doin' very well. But you see how we are now." There were two portraits--oil paintings--hanging against the wall. "Whose portraits are these?" said I. "Well; that's my master--an' this is me," replied she. "He would have 'em taken some time since. I couldn't think o' sellin' 'em; or else, yo see, we've sold nearly everything we had. I did try to pawn 'em, too, thinkin' we could get 'em back again when things came round; but, I can assure yo, I couldn't find a broker anywhere that would tak' 'em in." "Well, Missis," said my companion, "yo have one comfort; you are always clean." "Eh, bless yo!" replied she, "I couldn't live among dirt! My husban' tells me that I clean all the luck away; but aw'm sure there's no luck i' filth; if there is, anybody may tak' it for me."

The rain had stopt again; and after my friend had made a note respecting some additional relief for the family, we bade the woman good day. We had not gone far before a little ragged lass looked up admiringly at two pinks I had stuck in my buttonhole, and holding up her hand, said, "Eh, gi' me a posy!" My friend pointed to one of the cottages we passed, and said that the last time he called there, he found the family all seated round a large bowl of porridge, made of Indian meal. This meal is sold at a penny a pound. He stopped at another cottage and said, "Here's a house where I always find them reading when I call. I know the people very well." He knocked and tried the latch, but there was nobody in. As we passed an open door, the pleasant smell of oatcake baking came suddenly upon me. It woke up many memories of days gone by. I saw through the window a stout, meal-dusted old woman, busy with her wooden ladle and baking-shovel at a brisk oven. "Now, I should like to look in there for a minute or two, if it can be done," said I. "Well," replied my friend, "this woman is not on our books; she gets her own living in the way you see. But come in; it will be all right; I know her very well." I was glad of that, for I wanted to have a chat with her, and to peep at the baking. "Good morning, Missis," said he; "how are you?" "Why, just in a middlin' way." "How long is this wet weather going to last, think you?" "Nay, there ye hev me fast;--but what brings ye here this mornin'?" said the old woman, resting the end of her ladle on the little counter; "I never trouble sic like chaps as ye." "No, no," replied my friend; "we have not called about anything of that kind." "What, then, pray ye?" "Well, my friend, here, is almost a stranger in Preston; and as soon as ever he smelt the baking, he said he should like to see it, so I took the liberty of bringing him in." "Oh, ay; come in, an' welcome. Ye're just i' time, too; for I've bin sat at t' back to sarra (serve) t' pigs." "You're not a native of Lancashire, Missis," said I. "Why, wheer then? come, now; let's be knowin', as ye're so sharp." "Cumberland," said I. "Well, now; ye're reight, sewer enough. But how did ye find it out, now?" "Why, you said that you had been out to sarra t' pigs. A native of Lancashire would have said 'serve' instead of 'sarra.'" "Well, that's varra queer; for I've bin a lang time away from my awn country. But, whereivver do ye belang to, as ye're so bowd wi' me?" said she, smiling, and turning over a cake which was baking upon the oven. I told her that I was born a few miles from Manchester. "Manchester! never, sewer;" said she, resting her ladle again; "why, I lived ever so long i' Manchester when I was young. I was cook at th' Swan i' Shudehill, aboon forty year sin." She said that, in those days, the Swan, in Shudehill, was much frequented by the commercial men of Manchester. It was a favourite dining house for them. Many of them even brought their own beefsteak on a skewer; and paid a penny for the cooking of it. She said she always liked Manchester very well; but she had not been there for a good while. "But," said she, "ye'll hev plenty o' oatcake theer--sartin." "Not much, now," replied I; "it's getting out o' fashion." I told her that we had to get it once a week from a man who came all the way from Stretford into Manchester, with a large basketful upon his head, crying "Woat cakes, two a penny!" "Two a penny!" said she; "why, they'll not be near as big as these, belike." "Not quite," replied I. "Not quite! naw; not hauf t' size, aw warnd! Why, th' poor fellow desarves his brass iv he niver gev a farthin' for th' stuff to mak 'eni on. What! I knaw what oatcake bakin' is."

Leaving the canny old Cumberland woman at her baking, we called at a cottage in Everton Gardens. It was as clean as a gentleman's parlour; but there was no furniture in sight except a table, and, upon the table, a fine bush of fresh hawthorn blossom, stuck in a pint jug full of water. Here, I heard again the common story--they had been several months out of work; their household goods had dribbled away in ruinous sales, for something to live upon; and now, they had very little left but the walls. The little woman said to me, "Bless yo, there is at thinks we need'n nought, becose we keepen a daycent eawtside. But, I know my own know abeawt that. Beside, one doesn't like to fill folk's meawths, iv one is ill off."

It was now a little past noon, and we spent a few minutes looking through the Catholic schoolhouse, in Trinity Ward--a spacious brick building. The scholars were away at dinner. My friend is master of the school. His assistant offered to go with us to one or two Irish families in a close wynd, hard by, called Wilkie's Court. In every case I had the great advantage of being thus accompanied by gentlemen who were friendly and familiar with the poor we visited. This was a great facility to me. Wilkie's Court is a little cul de sac, with about half-a-dozen wretched cottages in it, fronted by a dead wall. The inhabitants of the place are all Irish. They were nearly all kept alive by relief from one source or other; but their poverty was not relieved by that cleanliness which I had witnessed in so many equally poor houses, making the best use of those simple means of comfort which are invaluable, although they cost little or nothing. In the first house we called at, a middle-aged woman was pacing slowly about the unwholesome house with a child in her arms. My friend inquired where the children were. "They are in the houses about; all but the one poor boy." "And where is he?" said I. "Well, he comes home now an' agin; he comes an' goes; sure, we don't know how. . . . Ah, thin, sir," continued she, beginning to cry, "I'll tell ye the rale truth, now. He was drawn away by some bad lads, an' he got three months in the New Bailey; that's God's truth. . . . Ah, what'll I do wid him," said she, bursting into tears afresh; "what'll I do wid him? sure, he is my own!" We did not stop long to intrude upon such trouble as this. She called out as we came away to tell us that the poor crayter next door was quite helpless. The next house was, in some respects, more comfortable than the last, though it was quite as poor in household goods. There was one flimsy deal table, one little chair, and two half-penny pictures of Catholic saints pinned against the wall. "Sure, I sold the other table since you wor here before," said the woman to my friend; "I sold it for two-an'-aightpence, an' bought this one for sixpence." At the house of another Irish family, my friend inquired where all the chairs were gone. "Oh," said a young woman," the baillies did fetch uvverything away, barrin' the one sate, when we were livin' in Lancaster Street." "Where do you all sit now, then?" "My mother sits there," replied she, "an' we sit upon the flure." "I heard they were goin' to sell these heawses," said one of the lads, "but, begorra," continued he, with a laugh, "I wouldn't wonder did they sell the ground from under us next." In the course of our visitation a thunder storm came on, during which we took shelter with a poor widow woman, who had a plateful of steeped peas for sale, in the window. She also dealt in rags and bones in a small way, and so managed to get a living, as she said, "beawt troublin' onybody for charity." She said it was a thing that folk had to wait a good deal out in the cold for.

It was market-day, and there were many country people in Preston. On my way back to the middle of the town, I called at an old inn, in Friargate, where I listened with pleasure a few minutes to the old-fashioned talk of three farmers from the Fylde country. Their conversation was principally upon cow-drinks. One of them said there was nothing in the world like "peppermint tay an' new butter" for cows that had the belly-ache. "They'll be reet in a varra few minutes at after yo gotten that into 'em," said he. As evening came on the weather settled into one continuous shower, and I left Preston in the heavy rain, weary, and thinking of what I had seen during the day. Since then I have visited the town again, and I shall say something about that visit hereafter.

CHAPTER IX.

The rain had been falling heavily through the night. It was raw and gusty, and thick clouds were sailing wildly overhead, as I went to the first train for Preston. It was that time of morning when there is a lull in the streets of Manchester, between six and eight. The "knocker-up" had shouldered his long wand, and paddled home to bed again; and the little stalls, at which the early workman stops for his half-penny cup of coffee, were packing up. A cheerless morning, and the few people that were about looked damp and low spirited. I bought the day's paper, and tried to read it, as we flitted by the glimpses of dirty garret-life, through the forest of chimneys, gushing forth their thick morning fumes into the drizzly air, and over the dingy web of Salford streets. We rolled on through Pendleton, where the country is still trying to look green here and there, under increasing difficulties; but it was not till we came to where the green vale of Clifton open out, that I became quite reconciled to the weather. Before we were well out of sight of the ancient tower of Prestwich Church, the day brightened a little. The shifting folds of gloomy cloud began to glide asunder, and through the gauzy veils which lingered in the interspaces, there came a dim radiance which lighted up the rain-drops "lingering on the pointed thorns;" and the tall meadow grasses were swaying to and fro with their loads of liquid pearls, in courtesies full of exquisite grace, as we whirled along. I enjoyed the ride that raw morning, although the sky was all gloom again long before we came in sight of the Ribble.

I met my friend, in Preston, at half-past nine; and we started at once for another ramble amongst the poor, in a different part of Trinity Ward. We went first to a little court, behind Bell Street. There is only one house in the court, and it is known as "Th' Back Heawse." In this cottage the little house-things had escaped the ruin which I had witnessed in so many other places. There were two small tables, and three chairs; and there were a few pots and a pan or two. Upon the cornice there were two pot spaniels, and two painted stone apples; and, between them, there was a sailor waving a union jack, and a little pudgy pot man, for holding tobacco. On the windowsill there was a musk-plant; and, upon the table by the staircase, there was a rude cage, containing three young throstles. The place was tidy; and there was a kind-looking old couple inside. The old man stood at the table in the middle of the floor, washing the pots, and the old woman was wiping them, and putting them away. A little lad sat by the fire, thwittling at a piece of stick. The old man spoke very few words the whole time we were there, but he kept smiling and going on with his washing. The old woman was very civil, and rather shy at first; but we soon got into free talk together. She told me that she had borne thirteen children. Seven of them were dead; and the other six were all married, and all poor. "I have one son," said she; "he's a sailmaker. He's th' best off of any of 'em. But, Lord bless yo; he's not able to help us. He gets very little, and he has to pay a woman to nurse his sick wife. . . . This lad that's here,--he's a little grandson o' mine; he's one of my dowter's childer. He brings his meight with him every day, an' sleeps with us. They han bod one bed, yo see. His father hasn't had a stroke o' work sin Christmas. They're badly off. As for us--my husband has four days a week on th' moor,--that's 4s., an' we've 2s. a week to pay out o' that for rent. Yo may guess fro that, heaw we are. He should ha' been workin' on the moor today, but they've bin rain't off. We've no kind o' meight i' this house bod three-ha'poth o' peas; an' we've no firin'. He's just brokken up an owd cheer to heat th' watter wi'. (The old man smiled at this, as if he thought it was a good joke.) He helps me to wesh, an' sick like; an' yo' know, it's a good deal better than gooin' into bad company, isn't it? (Here the old man gave her a quiet, approving look, like a good little lad taking notice of his mother's advice.) Aw'm very glad of a bit o' help," continued she,"for aw'm not so terrible mich use, mysel'. Yo see; aw had a paralytic stroke seven year sin, an' we've not getten ower it. For two year aw hadn't a smite o' use all deawn this side. One arm an' one leg trail't quite helpless. Aw drunk for ever o' stuff for it. At last aw gat somethin' ov a yarb doctor. He said that he could cure me for a very trifle, an' he did me a deal o' good, sure enough. He nobbut charged me hauve-a-creawn. . . . We never knowed what it was to want a meal's meight till lately. We never had a penny off th' parish, nor never trouble't anybody till neaw. Aw wish times would mend, please God! . . . We once had a pig, an' was in a nice way o' gettin' a livin'. . . . When things began o' gooin' worse an' worse with us, we went to live in a cellar, at sixpence a week rent; and we made it very comfortable, too. We didn't go there because we liked th' place; but we thought nobody would know; an, we didn't care, so as we could put on till times mended, an' keep aat o' debt. But th' inspectors turned us out, an' we had to come here, an' pay 2s. a week. . . . Aw do NOT like to ask for charity, iv one could help it. They were givin' clothin' up at th' church a while sin', an' some o' th' neighbours wanted me to go an' ax for some singlets, ye see aw cannot do without flannels,--but aw couldn't put th' face on." Now, the young throstles in the cage by the staircase began to chirp one after another. "Yer yo at that! "said the old man, turning round to the cage; "yer yo at that! Nobbut three week owd!" "Yes," replied the old woman; "they belong to my grandson theer. He brought 'em in one day --neest an' all; an' poor nake't crayters they were. He's a great lad for birds." "He's no worse nor me for that," answered the old man; "aw use't to be terrible fond o' brids when aw wur yung."

After a little more talk, we bade the old couple good day, and went to peep at the cellar where they had crept stealthily away, for the sake of keeping their expenses close to their lessening income. The place was empty, and the door was open. It was a damp and cheerless little hole, down in the corner of a dirty court. We went next into Pole Street, and tried the door of a cottage where a widow woman lived with her children less than a week before. They were gone, and the house was cleared out. "They have had neither fire nor candle in that house for weeks past," said my companion. We then turned up a narrow entry, which was so dark and low overhead that my companion only told me just in time to "mind my hat!" There are several such entries leading out of Pole Street to little courts behind. Here we turned into a cold and nearly empty cottage, where a middle-aged woman sat nursing a sick child. She looked worn and ill herself, and she had sore eyes. She told me that the child was her daughter's. Her daughter's husband had died of asthma in the workhouse, about six weeks before. He had not "addled" a penny for twelve months before he died. She said, "We hed a varra good heawse i' Stanley Street once; but we hed to sell up an' creep hitherto. This heawse is 2s. 3d. a week; an' we mun pay it, or go into th' street. Aw nobbut owed him for one week, an' he said, 'Iv yo connot pay yo mun turn eawt for thoose 'at will do.' Aw did think o' gooin' to th' Board," continued she, "for a pair o' clogs. My een are bad; an' awm ill all o'er, an' it's wi' nought but gooin' weet o' my feet. My daughter's wortchin'. Hoo gets 5s. 6d. a week. We han to live an' pay th' rent, too, eawt o' that." I guessed, from the little paper pictures on the wall, that they were Catholics.

In another corner behind Pole Street, we called at a cottage of two rooms, each about three yards square. A brother and sister lived together here. They were each about fifty years of age. They had three female lodgers, factory operatives, out of work. The sister said that her brother had been round to the factories that morning, "Thinking that as it wur a pastime, there would haply be somebody off; but he couldn't yer o' nought." She said she got a trifle by charing, but not much now; for folks were "beginnin' to do it for theirsels." We now turned into Cunliffe Street, and called upon an Irish family there. It was a family of seven--an old tailor, and his wife and children. They had "dismissed the relief," as he expressed it, "because they got a bit o' work." The family was making a little living by ripping up old clothes, and turning the cloth to make it up afresh into lads' caps and other cheap things. The old man had had a great deal of trouble with his family. "I have one girl," said he, "who has bothered my mind a dale. She is under the influence o' bad advice. I had her on my hands for many months; an', after that, the furst week's wages she got, she up, an' cut stick, an' left me. I have another daughter, now nigh nineteen years of age. The trouble I have with her I am content with; because it can't be helped. The poor crayter hasn't the use of all her faculties. I have taken no end o' pains with her, but I can't get her to count twenty on her finger ends wid a whole life's tachein'. Fortune has turned her dark side to me this long time, now; and, bedad, iv it wasn't for contrivin', an' workin' hard to boot, I wouldn't be able to keep above the flood. I assure ye it goes agin me to trouble the gentlemen o' the Board; an' so long as I am able, I will not. I was born in King's County; an' I was once well off in the city of Waterford I once had 400 pounds in the bank. I seen the time I didn't drame of a cloudy day; but things take quare turns in this world. How-an-ever, since it's no better, thank God it's no worse. Sure, it's a long lane that has never a turn in it."

CHAPTER X.

"There's nob'dy but the Lord an' me That knows what I've to bide." --NATTERIN NAN.

The slipshod old tailor shuffled after us to the door, talking about the signs of the times. His frame was bowed with age and labour, and his shoulders drooped away. It was drawing near the time when the grasshopper would be a burden to him. A hard life had silently engraved its faithful records upon that furrowed face; but there was a cheerful ring in his voice which told of a hopeful spirit within him still. The old man's nostrils were dusty with snuff, and his poor garments hung about his shrunken form in the careless ease which is common to the tailor's shopboard. I could not help admiring the brave old wrinkled workman as he stood in the doorway talking about his secondhand trade, whilst the gusty wind fondled about in his thin gray hair. I took a friendly pinch from his little wooden box at parting, and left him to go on struggling with his troublesome family to "keep above the flood," by translating old clothes into new. We called at some other houses, where the features of life were so much the same that it is not necessary to say more than that the inhabitants were all workless, or nearly so, and all living upon the charitable provision which is the only thin plank between so many people and death, just now. In one house, where the furniture had been sold, the poor souls had brought a great stone into the place, and this was their only seat. In Cunliffe Street, we passed the cottage of a boilermaker, whom I had heard of before. His family was four in number. This was one of those cases of wholesome pride in which the family had struggled with extreme penury, seeking for work in vain, but never asking for charity, until their own poor neighbours were at last so moved with pity for their condition, that they drew the attention of the Relief Committee to it. The man accepted relief for one week, but after that, he declined receiving it any longer, because he had met with a promise of employment. But the promise failed him when the time came. The employer, who had promised, was himself disappointed of the expected work. After this; the boilermaker's family was compelled to fall back upon the Relief Committee's allowance. He who has never gone hungry about the world, with a strong love of independence in his heart, seeking eagerly for work from day to day, and coming home night after night to a foodless, fireless house, and a starving family, disappointed and desponding, with the gloom of destitution deepening around him, can never fully realise what the feelings of such a man may be from anything that mere words can tell.

In Park Road, we called at the house of a hand-loom weaver. I learnt, before we went in, that two families lived here, numbering together eight persons; and, though it was well known to the committee that they had suffered as severely as any on the relief list, yet their sufferings had been increased by the anonymous slanders of some ill-disposed neighbours. They were quiet, well- conducted working people; and these slanders had grieved them very much. I found the poor weaver's wife very sensitive on this subject. Man's inhumanity to man may be found among the poor sometimes. It is not every one who suffers that learns mercy from that suffering. As I have said before, the husband was a calico weaver on the hand- loom. He had to weave about seventy-three yards of a kind of check for 3s., and a full week's work rarely brought him more than 5s. It seems astonishing that a man should stick year after year to such labour as this. But there is a strong adhesiveness, mingled with timidity, in some men, which helps to keep them down. In the front room of the cottage there was not a single article of furniture left, so far as I can remember.

The weaver's wife was in the little kitchen, and, knowing the gentleman who was with me, she invited us forward. She was a wan woman, with sunken eyes, and she was not much under fifty years of age. Her scanty clothing was whole and clean. She must have been a very good-looking woman sometime, though she seemed to me as if long years of hard work and poor diet had sapped the foundations of her constitution; and there was a curious changeful blending of pallor and feverish flush upon that worn face. But, even in the physical ruins of her countenance, a pleasing expression lingered still. She was timid and quiet in her manner at first, as if wondering what we had come for; but she asked me to sit down. There was no seat for my friend, and he stood leaning against the wall, trying to get her into easy conversation. The little kitchen looked so cheerless and bare that dull morning that it reminded me again of a passage in that rude, racy song of the Lancashire weaver, "Jone o' Greenfeelt"--

"Owd Bill o' Dan's sent us th' baillies one day, For a shop-score aw owed him, at aw couldn't pay; But, he were too lat, for owd Billy at th' Bent Had sent th' tit an' cart, an' taen th' goods off for rent,-- They laft nought but th' owd stoo; It were seats for us two, An' on it keawr't Margit an' me.

"Then, th' baillies looked reawnd 'em as sly as a meawse, When they see'd at o'th goods had bin taen eawt o' th' heawse; Says tone chap to tother, 'O's gone,--thae may see,'-- Says aw, 'Lads, ne'er fret, for yo're welcome to me!' Then they made no moor do, But nipt up wi' owd stoo, An' we both letten thwack upo' th' flags.

"Then aw said to eawr Margit, while we're upo' the floor, 'We's never be lower i' this world, aw'm sure; Iv ever things awtern they're likely to mend, For aw think i' my heart that we're both at th' fur end; For meight we ban noan, Nor no looms to weighve on, An' egad, they're as good lost as fund.'"

We had something to do to get the weaver's wife to talk to us freely, and I believe the reason was, that, after the slanders they had been subject to, she harboured a sensitive fear lest anything like doubt should be cast upon her story. "Well, Mrs," said my friend, "let's see; how many are you altogether in this house?" "We're two families, yo know," replied she; "there's eight on us all altogether." "Well," continued he,"and how much have you coming in, now?" He had asked this question so oft before, and had so often received the same answer, that the poor soul began to wonder what was the meaning of it all. She looked at us silently, her wan face flushed, and then, with tears rising in her eyes, she said, tremulously, "Well, iv yo' cannot believe folk--" My friend stopped her at once, and said, "Nay, Mrs_, you must not think that I doubt your story. I know all about it; but my friend wanted me to let you tell it your own way. We have come here to do you good, if possible, and no harm. You don't need to fear that." "Oh, well," said she, slowly wiping her moist forehead, and looking relieved," but yo know, aw was very much put about o'er th' ill-natur't talk as somebody set eawt." "Take no notice of them," said my friend; "take no notice. I meet with such things every day." "Well," continued she," yo know heaw we're situated. We were nine months an' hesn't a stroke o' wark. Eawr wenches are gettin' a day for t' sick, neaw and then, but that's all. There's a brother o' mine lives with us,--he'd a been clemmed into th' grave but for th' relief; an' aw've been many a time an' hesn't put a bit i' my meawth fro mornin' to mornin' again. We've bin married twenty-four year; an' aw don't think at him an' me together has spent a shillin' i' drink all that time. Why, to tell yo truth, we never had nought to stir on. My husband does bod get varra little upo th' hand-loom i' th' best o' times--5s. a week or so. He weighves a sort o' check--seventy-three yards for 3s." The back door opened into a little damp yard, hemmed in by brick walls. Over in the next yard we could see a man bustling about, and singing in a loud voice, "Hard times come again no more." "Yon fellow doesn't care much about th' hard times, I think," said I. "Eh, naw," replied she. "He'll live where mony a one would dee, will yon. He has that little shop, next dur; an' he keeps sellin' a bit o' toffy, an' then singin' a bit, an' then sellin' a bit moor toffy,--an' he's as happy as a pig amung slutch."

Leaving the weaver's cottage, the rain came on, and we sat a few minutes with a young shoemaker, who was busy at his bench, doing a cobbling job. His wife was lying ill upstairs. He had been so short of work for some time past that he had been compelled to apply for relief. He complained that the cheap gutta percha shoes were hurting his trade. He said a pair of men's gutta percha shoes could be bought for 5s. 6d., whilst it would cost him 7s. 6d. for the materials alone to make a pair of men's shoes of. When the rain was over, we left his house, and as we went along I saw in a cottage window a printed paper containing these words, "Bitter beer. This beer is made of herbs and roots of the native country." I know that there are many poor people yet in Lancashire who use decoctions of herbs instead of tea--mint and balm are the favourite herbs for this purpose; but I could not imagine what this herb beer could be, at a halfpenny a bottle, unless it was made of nettles. At the cottage door there was about four-pennyworth of mauled garden stuff upon an old tray. There was nobody inside but a little ragged lass, who could not tell us what the beer was made of. She had only one drinking glass in the place, and that had a snip out of the rim. The beer was exceedingly bitter. We drank as we could, and then went into Pump Street, to the house of a "core-maker," a kind of labourer for moulders. The core-maker's wife was in. They had four children. The whole six had lived for thirteen weeks on 3s. 6d. a week. When work first began to fall off, the husband told the visitors who came to inquire into their condition, that he had a little money saved up, and he could manage a while. The family lived upon their savings as long as they lasted, and then were compelled to apply for relief, or "clem." It was not quite noon when we left this house, and my friend proposed that before we went farther we should call upon Mrs G_, an interesting old woman, in Cunliffe Street. We turned back to the place, and there we found

"In lowly shed, and mean attire, A matron old, whom we schoolmistress name, Who boasts unruly brats with birch to tame."

In a small room fronting the street, the mild old woman sat, with her bed in one corner, and her simple vassals ranged upon the forms around. Here, "with quaint arts," she swayed the giddy crowd of little imprisoned elves, whilst they fretted away their irksome schooltime, and unconsciously played their innocent prelude to the serious drama of life. As we approach the open door--

"The noises intermix'd, which thence resound, Do learning's little tenement betray; Where sits the dame disguised in look profound, And eyes her fairy throng, and turns her wheel around."

The venerable little woman had lived in this house fourteen years. She was seventy-three years of age, and a native of Limerick. She was educated at St Ann's School, in Dublin, and she had lived fourteen years in the service of a lady in that city. The old dame made an effort to raise her feeble form when we entered, and she received us as courteously as the finest lady in the land could have done. She told us that she charged only a penny a-week for her teaching; but, said she, "some of them can't pay it." "There's a poor child," continued she, "his father has been out of work eleven months, and they are starving but for the relief. Still, I do get a little, and I like to have the children about me. Oh, my case is not the worst, I know. I have people lodging in the house who are not so well off as me. I have three families living here. One is a family of four; they have only 3s. a-week to live upon. Another is a family of three; they have 6s. a-week from a club, but they pay me 2s. a- week. for rent out of that. . . . . I am very much troubled with my eyes; my sight is failing fast. If I drop a stitch when I'm knitting, I can't see to take it up again. If I could buy a pair of spectacles, they would help me a good dale; but I cannot afford till times are better." I could not help thinking how many kind souls there are in the world who would be glad to give the old woman a pair of spectacles, if they knew her.

CHAPTER XI.

We talked with the old schoolmistress in Cunliffe Street till it was "high twelve" at noon, and then the kind jailer of learning's little prison-house let all her fretful captives go. The clamorous elves rushed through the doorway into the street, like a stream too big for its vent, rejoicing in their new-found freedom and the open face of day. The buzz of the little teaching mill was hushed once more, and the old dame laid her knitting down, and quietly wiped her weak and weary eyes. The daughters of music were brought low with her, but, in the last thin treble of second childhood, she trembled forth mild complaints of her neighbours' troubles, but very little of her own. We left her to enjoy her frugal meal and her noontide reprieve in peace, and came back to the middle of the town. On our way I noticed again some features of street life which are more common in manufacturing towns just now than when times are good. Now and then one meets with a man in the dress of a factory worker selling newspapers, or religious tracts, or back numbers of the penny periodicals, which do not cost much. It is easy to see, from their shy and awkward manner, that they are new to the trade, and do not like it. They are far less dexterous, and much more easily "said," than the brisk young salesmen who hawk newspapers in the streets of Manchester. I know that many of these are unemployed operatives trying to make an honest penny in this manner till better days return. Now and then, too, a grown-up girl trails along the street, "with wandering steps and slow," ragged, and soiled, and starved, and looking as if she had travelled far in the rainy weather, houseless and forlorn. I know that such sights may be seen at any time, but not near so often as just now; and I cannot help thinking that many of these are poor sheep which have strayed away from the broken folds of labour. Sometimes it is an older woman that goes by, with a child at the breast, and one or two holding by the skirt of her tattered gown, and perhaps one or two more limping after, as she crawls along the pavement, gazing languidly from side to side among the heedless crowd, as if giving her last look round the world for help, without knowing where to get it, and without heart to ask for it. It is easy to give wholesale reasons why nobody needs to be in such a condition as this; but it is not improbable that there are some poor souls who, from no fault of their own, drop through the great sieve of charity into utter destitution. "They are well kept that God keeps." May the continual dew of Heaven's blessing gladden the hearts of those who deal kindly with them!

After dinner I fell into company with some gentlemen who were talking about the coming guild--that ancient local festival, which is so clear to the people of Preston, that they are not likely to allow it to go by wholly unhonoured, however severe the times may be. Amongst them was a gray-haired friend of mine, who is a genuine humorist. He told us many quaint anecdotes. One of them was of a man who went to inquire the price of graves in a certain cemetery. The sexton told him that they were 1 pound on this side, and 2 pounds on the other side of the knoll. "How is it that they are 2 pounds on the other side?" inquired the man. "Well, becose there's a better view there," replied the sexton. There were three or four millowners in the company, and, when the conversation turned upon the state of trade, one of them said, "I admit that there is a great deal of distress, but we are not so badly off yet as to drive the operatives to work for reasonable wages. For instance, I had a labourer working for me at 10s. a-week; he threw up my employ, and went to work upon the moor for 1s. a-day. How do you account for that? And then, again, I had another man employed as a watchman and roller coverer, at 18s. a-week. I found that I couldn't afford to keep him on at 18s., so I offered him 15s. a-week; but he left it, and went to work on the moor at 1s. a-day; and, just now, I want a man to take his place, and cannot get one." Another said, "I am only giving low wages to my workpeople, but they get more with me than they can make on the moor, and yet I cannot keep them." I heard some other things of the same kind, for which there might be special reasons; but these gentlemen admitted the general prevalence of severe distress, and the likelihood of its becoming much worse.

At two o'clock I sallied forth again, under convoy of another member of the Relief Committee, into the neighbourhood of Messrs Horrocks, Miller, and Co.'s works. Their mill is known as "Th' Yard Factory." Hereabouts the people generally are not so much reduced as in some parts of the town, because they have had more employment, until lately, than has been common elsewhere. But our business lay with those distressed families who were in receipt of relief, and, even here, they were very easy to find. The first house we called at was inhabited by a family of five--man and wife and three children. The man was working on the moor at one shilling a-day. The wife was unwell, but she was moving about the house. They had buried one girl three weeks before; and one of the three remaining children lay ill of the measles. They had suffered a great deal from sickness. The wife said, "My husband is a peawer-loom weighver. He had to come whoam ill fro' his wark; an' then they shopped his looms, (gave his work to somebody else,) an' he couldn't get 'em back again. He'll get 'em back as soon as he con, yo may depend; for we don't want to bother folk for no mak o' relief no lunger than we can help." In addition to the husband's pay upon the moor, they were receiving 2s. a week from the Committee, making altogether 8s. a week for the five, with 2s. 6d. to pay out of it for rent. She said, "We would rayther ha' soup than coffee, becose there's moor heytin' in it." My friend looked in at the door of a cottage in Barton Street. There was a sickly-looking woman inside. "Well, missis," said my friend, jocularly, "how are you? because, if you're ill, I've brought a doctor here." "Eh," replied she, "aw could be ill in a minute, if aw could afford, but these times winnot ston doctors' bills. Besides, aw never were partial to doctors' physic; it's kitchen physic at aw want. Han yo ony o' that mak' wi' yo?" She said," My husban' were th' o'erlooker o' th'weighvers at "Owd Tom's.' They stopt to fettle th' engine a while back, an' they'n never started sin'. But aw guess they wi'n do some day." We had not many yards to go to the next place, which was a poor cottage in Fletcher's Row, where a family of eight persons resided. There was very little furniture in the place, but I noticed a small shelf of books in a corner by the window. A feeble woman, upwards of seventy years old, sat upon a stool tending the cradle of a sleeping infant. This infant was the youngest of five children, the oldest of the five was seven years of age. The mother of the three-weeks-old infant had just gone out to the mill to claim her work from the person who had been filling her place during her confinement. The old woman said that the husband was "a grinder in a card-room when they geet wed, an' he addled about 8s. a week; but, after they geet wed, his wife larn't him to weighve upo' th' peawer-looms." She said that she was no relation to them, but she nursed, and looked after the house for them. "They connot afford to pay mo nought," continued she, "but aw fare as they fare'n, an' they dunnot want to part wi' me. Aw'm not good to mich, but aw can manage what they wanten, yo see'n. Aw never trouble't noather teawn nor country i' my life, an' aw hope aw never shall for the bit o' time aw have to do on." She said that the Board of Guardians had allowed the family 10s. a week for the two first weeks of the wife's confinement, but now their income amounted to a little less than one shilling a head per week.

Leaving this house, we turned round the corner into St Mary's Street North. Here we found a clean-looking young working man standing shivering by a cottage door, with his hands in his pockets. He was dressed in well-mended fustian, and he had a cloth cap on his head. His face had a healthy hunger-nipt look. "Hollo," said my friend, "I thought you was working on the moor." "Ay," replied the young man, "Aw have bin, but we'n bin rain't off this afternoon." "Is there nobody in?" said my friend. "Naw, my wife's gone eawt; hoo'll not be mony minutes. Hoo's here neaw." A clean little pale woman came up, with a child in her arms, and we went in. They had not much furniture in the small kitchen, which was the only place we saw, but everything was sweet and orderly. Their income was, as usual in relief cases, about one shilling a head per week. "You had some lodgers," said my friend. "Ay," said she,"but they're gone." "How's that?" "We had a few words. Their little lad was makin' a great noise i' the passage theer, an' aw were very ill o' my yed, an' aw towd him to go an' play him at tother side o' th' street,--so, they took it amiss, an' went to lodge wi' some folk i' Ribbleton Lone."

We called at another house in this street. A family of six lived there. The only furniture I saw in the place was two chairs, a table, a large stool, a cheap clock, and a few pots. The man and his wife were in. She was washing. The man was a stiff built, shock- headed little fellow, with a squint in his eye that seemed to enrich the good-humoured expression of his countenance. Sitting smiling by the window, he looked as if he had lots of fun in him, if he only had a fair chance of letting it off. He told us that he was a "tackler" by trade. A tackler is one who fettles looms when they get out of order. "Couldn't you get on at Horrocks's?" said my friend. "Naw," replied he; "they'n not ha' men-weighvers theer." The wife said," We're a deal better off than some. He has six days a week upo th' moor, an' we'n 3s. a week fro th' Relief Committee. We'n 2s. 6d. a week to pay eawt on it for rent; but then, we'n a lad that gets 4d. a day neaw an' then for puttin' bobbins on; an' every little makes a mickle, yo known." "How is it that your clock's stopt?" said I. "Nay," said the little fellow; "aw don't know. Want o' cotton, happen,--same as everything else is stopt for." Leaving this house we met with another member of the Relief Committee, who was overlooker of a mill a little way off. I parted here with the gentleman who had accompanied me hitherto, and the overlooker went on with me.

In Newton Street he stopped, and said, "Let's look in here." We went up two steps, and met a young woman coming out at the cottage door. "How's Ruth?" said my friend. "Well, hoo is here. Hoo's busy bakin' for Betty." We went in. "You're not bakin' for yourselves, then?" said he. "Eh, naw," replied the young woman," it's mony a year sin' we had a bakin' o' fleawr, isn't it, Ruth?" The old woman who was baking turned round and said, "Ay; an' it'll be mony another afore we han one aw deawt." There were three dirty-looking hens picking and croodling about the cottage floor. "How is it you don't sell these, or else eat 'em?" said he. "Eh, dear," replied the old woman, "dun yo want mo kilt? He's had thoose hens mony a year; an' they rooten abeawt th' heawse just th' same as greadley Christians. He did gi' consent for one on 'em to be kilt yesterday; but aw'll be hanged iv th' owd cracky didn't cry like a chylt when he see'd it beawt yed. He'd as soon part wi' one o'th childer as one o'th hens. He says they're so mich like owd friends, neaw. He's as quare as Dick's hat-bant 'at went nine times reawnd an' wouldn't tee. . . . We thought we'd getten a shop for yon lad o' mine t'other day. We yerd ov a chap at Lytham at wanted a lad to tak care o' six jackasses an' a pony. Th' pony were to tak th' quality to Blackpool, and such like. So we fettled th' lad's bits o' clooas up and made him ever so daycent, and set him off to try to get on wi' th' chap at Lytham. Well, th' lad were i' good heart abeawt it; an' when he geet theer th' chap towd him at he thought he wur very likely for th' job, so that made it better,--an' th' lad begun o' wearin' his bit o' brass o' summat to eat, an' sich like, thinkin' he're sure o' th' shop. Well, they kept him there, dallyin', aw tell yo, an' never tellin' him a greadley tale, fro Sunday till Monday o' th' neet, an' then,--lo an' behold,--th' mon towd him that he'd hire't another; and th' lad had to come trailin' whoam again, quite deawn i'th' meawth. Eh, aw wur some mad! Iv aw'd been at th' back o' that chap, aw could ha' punce't him, see yo!" "Well," said my friend, "there's no work yet, Ruth, is there?" "Wark! naw; nor never will be no moor, aw believe." "Hello, Ruth!" said the young woman, pointing through the window, "dun yo know who yon is?" "Know? ay," replied the old woman; "He's getten aboon porritch neaw, has yon. He walks by me i'th street, as peart as a pynot, an' never cheeps. But, he's no 'casion. Aw know'd him when his yure stickt out at top ov his hat; and his shurt would ha' hanged eawt beheend, too,--like a Wigan lantron,--iv he'd had a shurt."

CHAPTER XII.

"Oh, reason not the deed; our basest beggars Are in the poorest things superfluous: Allow not nature more than nature needs, Man's life is cheap as beast's." --King Lear.

A short fit of rain came on whilst we were in the cottage in Newton Street, so we sat a little while with Ruth, listening to her quaint tattle about the old man and his feathered pets; about the children, the hard times, and her own personal ailments;--for, though I could not help thinking her a very good-hearted, humorous old woman, bravely disposed to fight it out with the troubles of her humble lot, yet it was clear that she was inclined to ease her harassed mind now and then by a little wholesome grumbling; and I dare say that sometimes she might lose her balance so far as to think, like "Natterin' Nan," "No livin' soul atop o't earth's bin tried as I've bin tried:

there's nob'dy but the Lord an' me that knows what I've to bide."

Old age and infirmity, too, had found Ruth out, in her penurious obscurity; and she was disposed to complain a little, like Nan, sometimes, of "the ills that flesh is heir to:"-

"Fro' t' wind i't stomach, rheumatism, Tengin pains i't gooms, An' coughs, an' cowds, an' t' spine o't back, I suffer martyrdom.

"Yet nob'dy pities mo, or thinks I'm ailin' owt at all; T' poor slave mun tug an' tew wi't wark, Wolivver shoo can crawl."

Old Ruth was far from being as nattle and querulous as the famous ill-natured grumbler so racily pictured by Benjamin Preston, of Bradford; but, like most of the dwellers upon earth, she was a little bit touched with the same complaint. When the rain was over, we came away. I cannot say that the weather ever "cleared up" that day; for, at the end of every shower, the dark, slow-moving clouds always seemed to be mustering for another downfall. We came away, and left the "cant" old body "busy bakin' for Betty," and "shooing" the hens away from her feet, and she shuffled about the house. A few yards lower in Newton Street, we turned up a low, dark entry, which led to a gloomy little court behind. This was one of those unhealthy, pent-up cloisters, where misery stagnates and broods among the "foul congregation of pestilential vapours" which haunt the backdoor life of the poorest parts of great towns. Here, those viewless ministers of health--the fresh winds of heaven--had no free play; and poor human nature inhaled destruction from the poisonous effluvia that festered there. And, in such nooks as this, there may be found many decent working people, who have been accustomed to live a cleanly life in their humble way in healthy quarters, now reduced to extreme penury, pinching, and pining, and nursing the flickering hope of better days, which may enable them to flee from the foul harbour which strong necessity has driven them to. The dark aspect of the day filled the court with a tomb-like gloom. If I remember aright, there were only three or four cottages in it. We called at two of them. Before we entered the first, my friend said, "A young couple lives here. They are very decent people. They have not been here long; and they have gone through a great deal before they came here." There were two or three pot ornaments on the cornice; but there was no furniture in the place, save one chair, which was occupied by a pale young woman, nursing her child. Her thin, intelligent face looked very sad. Her clothing, though poor, was remarkably clean; and, as she sat there, in the gloomy, fireless house, she said very little, and what she said she said very quietly, as if she had hardly strength to complain, and was even half-ashamed to do so. She told us, however, that her husband had been out of work six months. "He didn't know what to turn to after we sowd th' things," said she; "but he's takken to cheer-bottomin', for he doesn't want to lie upo' folk for relief, if he can help it. He doesn't get much above a cheer, or happen two in a week, one week wi' another, an' even then he doesn't olez get paid, for folks ha' not brass. It runs very hard with us, an' I'm nobbut sickly." The poor soul did not need to say much; her own person, which evinced such a touching struggle to keep up a decent appearance to the last, and everything about her, as she sat there in the gloomy place, trying to keep the child warm upon her cold breast, told eloquently what her tongue faltered at and failed to express.

The next place we called at in this court was a cottage kept by a withered old woman, with one foot in the grave. We found her in the house, sallow, and shrivelled, and panting for breath. She had three young women, out of work, lodging with her; and, in addition to these, a widow with her two children lived there. One of these children, a girl, was earning 2s. 6d. a week for working short time at a mill; the other, a lad, was earning 3s. a week. The rest were all unemployed, and had been so for several months past. This 5s. 6d. a week was all the seven people had to live upon, with the exception of a trifle the sickly old woman received from the Board of Guardians. As we left the court, two young fellows were lounging at the entry end, as if waiting for us. One of them stepped up to my friend, and whispered something plaintively, pointing to his feet. I did not catch the reply; but my friend made a note, and we went on. Before we had gone many yards down the street a storm of rain and thunder came on, and we hurried into the house of an old Irishwoman close by. My friend knew the old woman. She was on his list of relief cases. "Will you let us shelter a few minutes, Mrs _?" said he. "I will, an' thank ye," replied she. "Come in an' sit down. Sure, it's not fit to turn out a dog. Faith, that's a great storm. Oh, see the rain! Thank God it's not him that made the house that made the pot! Dear, dear; did ye see the awful flash that time? I don't like to be by myself, I am so terrified wi' the thunder. There has been a great dale o' wet this long time." "There, has," replied my friend; "but how have ye been getting on since I called before?" "Well," said the old woman, sitting down, "things is quare with us as ever they can be, an' that you know very well." There was a young woman reared against the table by the window. My friend turned towards her, and said, "Well, and how does the Indian meal agree with you?" The young woman blushed, and smiled, but said nothing; but the old woman turned sharply round and replied, "Well, now, it is better nor starvation; it is chape, an' it fills up--an' that's all." "Is your son working?" inquired my friend. "Troth, he is," replied she. "He does be gettin' a day now an' again at the breek-croft in Ribbleton Lone. Faith, it is time he did somethin', too, for he was nine months out o' work entirely. I am got greatly into debt, an' I don't think I'll ever be able to get over it any more. I don't know how does poor folk be able to spind money on drink such times as thim; bedad, I cannot do it. It is bard enough to get mate of any kind to keep the bare life in a body. Oh, see now; but for the relief, the half o' the country would die out." "You're a native of Ireland, missis," said I. "Troth, I am," replied she; "an' had a good farm o' greawnd in it too, one time. Ah! many's the dark day I went through between that an' this. Before thim bad times came on, long ago, people were well off in ould Ireland. I seen them wid as many as tin cows standin' at the door at one time. . . . Ah, then! but the Irish people is greatly scattered now! . . . But, for the matter of that, folk are as badly off here as anywhere in the world, I think. I dunno know how does poor folk be able to spind money for dhrink. I am a widow this seventeen year now, an' the divle a man or woman uvver seen me goin' to a public-house. I seen women goin' a drinkin' widout a shift to their backs. I dunno how the divvle they done it. Begorra, I think, if I drunk a glass of ale just now, my two legs would fail from under me immadiately--I am that wake." The old woman was a little too censorious, I think. There is no doubt that even people who are starving do drink a little sometimes. The wonder would be if they did not, in some degree, share the follies of the rest of the world. Besides, it is a well-known fact, that those who are in employ, are apt, from a feeling of misdirected kindness, to treat those who are out of work to a glass of ale or two, now and then; and it is very natural, too, that those who have been but ill-fed for a long time are not able to stand it well.

After leaving the old Irishwoman's house, we called upon a man who had got his living by the sale of newspapers. There was nothing specially worthy of remark in this case, except that he complained of his trade having fallen away a good deal. "I used to sell three papers where I now sell one," said he. This may not arise from there being fewer papers sold, but from there being more people selling them than when times were good. I came back to Manchester in the evening. I have visited Preston again since then, and have spent some time upon Preston Moor, where there are nearly fifteen hundred men, principally factory operatives, at work. Of this I shall have something to say in my next paper.

CHAPTER XIII.

'The rose of Lancaster for lack of nurture pales." --
BLACKBURN BARD.

It was early on a fine morning in July when I next set off to see Preston again; the long-continued rains seemed to be ended, and the unclouded sun flooded all the landscape with splendour. All nature rejoiced in the change, and the heart of man was glad. In Clifton Vale, the white-sleeved mowers were at work among the rich grass, and the scent of new hay came sweetly through our carriage windows. In the leafy cloughs and hedges, the small birds were wild with joy, and every garden sent forth a goodly smell. Along its romantic vale the glittering Irwell meandered, here, through nooks, "o'erhung wi' wildwoods, thickening green;" and there, among lush unshaded pastures; gathering on its way many a mild whispering brook, whose sunlit waters laced the green land with freakish lines of trembling gold. To me this ride is always interesting, so many points of historic interest line the way; but it was doubly delightful on that glorious July morning. And I never saw Fishergate, in Preston, look better than it did then. On my arrival there I called upon the Secretary of the Trinity Ward Relief Committee. In a quiet bye- street, where there are four pleasant cottages, with little gardens in front of them, I found him in his studious nook, among books, relief tickets, and correspondence. We had a few minutes' talk about the increasing distress of the town; and he gave me a short account of the workroom which has been opened in Knowsley Street, for the employment of female factory operatives out of work. This workroom is managed by a committee of ladies, some of whom are in attendance every day. The young women are employed upon plain sewing. They have two days' work a week, at one shilling a day, and the Relief Committee adds sixpence to this 2s. in each case. Most of them are merely learning to sew. Many of them prove to be wholly untrained to this simple domestic accomplishment. The work is not remunerative, nor is it expected to be so; but the benefit which may grow out of the teaching which these young women get here--and the evil their employment here may prevent, cannot be calculated. I find that such workrooms are established in some of the other towns now suffering from the depression of trade. Some of these I intend to visit hereafter. I spent an interesting half-hour with the secretary, after which I went to see the factory operatives at work upon Preston Moor.

Preston Moor is a tract of waste land on the western edge of the town. It belongs to the corporation. A little vale runs through a great part of this moor, from south-east to north-west; and the ground was, until lately, altogether uneven. On the town side of the little dividing vale the land is a light, sandy soil; on the other side, there is abundance of clay for brickmaking. Upon this moor there are now fifteen hundred men, chiefly factory operatives, at work, levelling the land for building purposes, and making a great main sewer for the drainage of future streets. The men, being almost all unused to this kind of labour, are paid only one shilling per day; and the whole scheme has been devised for the employment of those who are suffering from the present depression of trade. The work had been going on several months before I saw it, and a great part of the land was levelled. When I came in sight of the men, working in scattered gangs that fine morning, there was, as might be expected, a visible difference between their motions and those of trained "navvies" engaged upon the same kind of labour. There were also very great differences of age and physical condition amongst them--old men and consumptive-looking lads, hardly out of their teens. They looked hard at me as I walked down the central line, but they were not anyway uncivil. "What time is 't, maister?"

asked a middle-aged man, with gray hair, as he wiped his forehead. "Hauve- past ten," said I. "What time says he?" inquired a feeble young fellow, who was resting upon his barrow. "Hauve-past ten, he says," replied the other. "Eh; it's warm!" said the tired lad, lying down upon his barrow again. One thing I noticed amongst these men, with very rare exceptions, their apparel, however poor, evinced that wholesome English love of order and cleanliness which generally indicates something of self-respect in the wearer--especially among poor folk. There is something touching in the whiteness of a well- worn shirt, and the careful patches of a poor man's old fustian coat.

As I lounged about amongst the men, a mild-eyed policeman came up, and offered to conduct me to Jackson, the labour-master, who had gone down to the other end of the moor, to look after the men at work at the great sewer--a wet clay cutting--the heaviest bit of work on the ground. We passed some busy brickmakers, all plastered and splashed with wet clay --of the earth, earthy. Unlike the factory operatives around them, these men clashed, and kneaded, and sliced among the clay, as if they were working for a wager. But they were used to the job, and working piece-work. A little further on, we came to an unbroken bit of the moor. Here, on a green slope we saw a poor lad sitting chirruping upon the grass, with a little cloutful of groundsel for bird meat in his hand, watching another, who was on his knees, delving for earth-nuts with an old knife. Lower down the slope there were three other lads plaguing a young jackass colt; and further off, on the town edge of the moor, several children from the streets hard by, were wandering about the green hollow, picking daisies, and playing together in the sunshine. There are several cotton factories close to the moor, but they were quiet enough. Whilst I looked about me here, the policeman pointed to the distance and said, "Jackson's comin' up, I see. Yon's him, wi' th' white lin' jacket on." Jackson seems to have won the esteem of the men upon the moor by his judicious management and calm determination. I have heard that he had a little trouble at first, through an injurious report spread amongst the men immediately before he undertook the management. Some person previously employed upon the ground had "set it eawt that there wur a chap comin' that would make 'em addle a hauve-a-creawn a day for their shillin'." Of course this increased the difficulty of his position; but he seems to have fought handsomely through all that sort of thing. I had met him for a few minutes once before, so there was no difficulty between us.

"Well, Jackson," said I, "heaw are yo gettin' on among it?" "Oh, very well, very well," said he," We'n more men at work than we had, an' we shall happen have more yet. But we'n getten things into something like system, an' then tak 'em one with another th' chaps are willin' enough. You see they're not men that have getten a livin' by idling aforetime; they're workin' men, but they're strange to this job, an' one cannot expect 'em to work like trained honds, no moor than one could expect a lot o' navvies to work weel at factory wark. Oh, they done middlin', tak 'em one with another." I now asked him if he had not had some trouble with the men at first. "Well," said he, "I had at first, an' that's the truth. I remember th' first day that I came to th' job. As I walked on to th' ground there was a great lump o' clay coom bang into my earhole th' first thing; but I walked on, an' took no notice, no moor than if it had bin a midge flyin' again my face. Well, that kind o' thing took place, now an' then, for two or three days, but I kept agate o' never mindin'; till I fund there were some things that I thought could be managed a deal better in a different way; so I gav' th' men notice that I would have 'em altered. For instance, now, when I coom here at first, there was a great shed in yon hollow; an' every mornin' th' men had to pass through that shed one after another, an' have their names booked for th' day. The result wur, that after they'd walked through th' shed, there was many on 'em walked out at t'other end o' th' moor straight into teawn a-playin' 'em. Well, I was determined to have that system done away with. An', when th' men fund that I was gooin' to make these alterations, they growled a good deal, you may depend, an' two or three on 'em coom up an' spoke to me abeawt th' matter, while tother stood clustered a bit off. Well; I was beginnin' to tell 'em plain an' straight-forrud what I would have done, when one o' these three sheawted out to th' whole lot, "Here, chaps, come an' gether reawnd th' devil. Let's yer what he's for!" 'Well,' said I, 'come on, an' you shall yer,' for aw felt cawmer just then, than I did when it were o'er. There they were, gethered reawnd me in a minute,--th' whole lot,--I were fair hemmed in. But I geet atop ov a bit ov a knowe, an' towd 'em a fair tale,-- what I wanted, an' what I would have, an' I put it to 'em whether they didn't consider it reet. An' I believe they see'd th' thing in a reet leet, but they said nought about it, but went back to their wark, lookin' sulky. But I've had very little bother with 'em sin'. I never see'd a lot o' chaps so altered sin' th' last February, as they are. At that time no mortal mon hardly could walk through 'em 'beawt havin' a bit o' slack-jaw, or a lump o' clay or summat flung a-him. But it isn't so, neaw. I consider th' men are doin' very weel. But, come; yo mun go deawn wi' me a-lookin' at yon main sewer."

CHAPTER XIV.

"Oh, let us bear the present as we may, Nor let the golden past be all forgot; Hope lifts the curtain of the future day, Where peace and plenty smile without a spot On their white garments; where the human lot Looks lovelier and less removed from heaven; Where want, and war, and discord enter not, But that for which the wise have hoped and striven-- The wealth of happiness, to humble worth is given.

'The time will come, as come again it must, When Lancashire shall lift her head once more; Her suffering sons, now down amid the dust Of Indigence, shall pass through Plenty's door; Her commerce cover seas from shore to shore; Her arts arise to highest eminence; Her products prove unrivall'd, as of yore; Her valour and her virtue--men of sense And blue-eyed beauties--England's pride and her defence." --BLACKBURN BARD.

Jackson's office as labour-master kept him constantly tramping about the sandy moor from one point to another. He was forced to be in sight, and on the move, during working hours, amongst his fifteen hundred scattered workmen. It was heavy walking, even in dry weather; and as we kneaded through the loose soil that hot forenoon, we wiped our foreheads now and then. "Ay," said he, halting, and looking round upon the scene, "I can assure you, that when I first took howd o' this job, I fund my honds full, as quiet as it looks now. I was laid up for nearly a week, an' I had to have two doctors. But, as I'd undertakken the thing, I was determined to go through with it to th' best o' my ability; an' I have confidence now that we shall be able to feight through th' bad time wi' summat like satisfaction, so far as this job's consarned, though it's next to impossible to please everybody, do what one will. But come wi' me down this road. I've some men agate o' cuttin' a main sewer. It's very little farther than where th' cattle pens are i' th' hollow yonder; and it's different wark to what you see here. Th' main sewer will have to be brought clean across i' this direction, an' it'll be a stiffish job. Th' cattle market's goin' to be shifted out o' yon hollow, an' in another year or two th' whole scene about here will be changed." Jackson and I both remembered something of the troubles of the cotton manufacture in past times. We had seen something of the "shuttle gatherings," the "plug-drawings," the wild starvation riots, and strikes of days gone by; and he agreed with me that one reason for the difference of their demeanour during the present trying circumstances lies in their increasing intelligence. The great growth of free discussion through the cheap press has done no little to work out this salutary change. There is more of human sympathy, and of a perception of the union of interests between employers and employed than ever existed before in the history of the cotton trade. Employers know that their workpeople are human beings, of like feelings and passions with themselves, and like themselves, endowed with no mean degree of independent spirit and natural intelligence; and working men know better than beforetime that their employers are not all the heartless tyrants which it has been too fashionable to encourage them to believe. The working men have a better insight into the real causes of trade panics than they used to have; and both masters and men feel more every day that their fortunes are naturally bound together for good or evil; and if the working men of Lancashire continue to struggle through the present trying pass of their lives with the brave patience which they have shown hitherto, they will have done more to defeat the arguments of those who hold them to be unfit for political power than the finest eloquence of their best friends could have done in the same time.

The labour master and I had a little talk about these things as we went towards the lower end of the moor. A few minutes' slow walk brought us to the spot, where some twenty of the hardier sort of operatives were at work in a damp clay cutting. "This is heavy work for sich chaps as these," said Jackson; "but I let 'em work bi'th lump here. I give'em so much clay apiece to shift, and they can begin when they like, an' drop it th' same. Th' men seem satisfied wi' that arrangement, an' they done wonders, considerin' th' nature o'th job. There's many o'th men that come on to this moor are badly off for suitable things for their feet. I've had to give lots o' clogs away among'em. You see men cannot work with ony comfort among stuff o' this sort without summat substantial on. It rives poor shoon to pieces i' no time. Beside, they're not men that can ston bein' witchod (wetshod) like some. They haven't been used to it as a rule. Now, this is one o'th' finest days we've had this year; an' you haven't sin what th' ground is like in bad weather. But you'd be astonished what a difference wet makes on this moor. When it's bin rain for a day or two th' wark's as heavy again. Th' stuff's heavier to lift, an' worse to wheel; an' th' ground is slutchy. That tries 'em up, an' poo's their shoon to pieces; an' men that are wakely get knocked out o' time with it. But thoose that can stand it get hardened by it. There's a great difference; what would do one man's constitution good will kill another. Winter time 'll try 'em up tightly. . . Wait there a bit," continued he, "I'll be with you again directly." He then went down into the cutting to speak to some of his men, whilst I walked about the edge of the bank. From a distant part of the moor, the bray of a jackass came faint upon the sleepy wind. "Yer tho', Jone," said one of the men, resting upon his spade; "another cally-weighver gone!" " Ay," replied Jone, "th' owd lad's deawn't his cut. He'll want no more tickets, yon mon!" The country folk of Lancashire say that a weaver dies every time a jackass brays. Jackson came up from the cutting, and we walked back to where the greatest number of men were at work. "You should ha' bin here last Saturday," said he; "we'd rather a curious scene. One o' the men coom to me an' axed if I'd allow 'em hauve-an-hour to howd a meetin' about havin' a procession i' th' guild week. I gav' 'em consent, on condition that they'd conduct their meetin' in an orderly way. Well, they gethered together upo' that level theer; an' th' speakers stood upo' th' edge o' that cuttin', close to Charnock Fowd. Th' meetin' lasted abeawt a quarter ov an hour longer than I bargained for; but they lost no time wi' what they had to do. O' went off quietly; an' they finished with 'Rule Britannia,' i' full chorus, an' then went back to their wark. You'll see th' report in today's paper."

This meeting was so curious, and so characteristic of the men, that I think the report is worth repeating here:--"On Saturday afternoon, a meeting of the parish labourers was held on the moor, to consider the propriety of having a demonstration of their numbers on one day in the guild week. There were upwards of a thousand present. An operative, named John Houlker, was elected to conduct the proceedings. After stating the object of the assembly, a series of propositions were read to the meeting by William Gillow, to the effect that a procession take place of the parish labourers in the guild week; that no person be allowed to join in it except those whose names were on the books of the timekeepers; that no one should receive any of the benefits which might accrue who did not conduct himself in an orderly manner; that all persons joining the procession should be required to appear on the ground washed and shaven, and their clogs, shoes, and other clothes cleaned; that they were not expected to purchase or redeem any articles of clothing in order to take part in the demonstration; and that any one absenting himself from the procession should be expelled from any participation in the advantages which might arise from the subscriptions to be collected by their fellow-labourers. These were all agreed to, and a committee of twelve was appointed to collect subscriptions and donations. A president, secretary, and treasurer were also elected, and a number of resolutions agreed to in reference to the carrying out of the details of their scheme. The managing committee consist of Messrs W. Gillow, Robert Upton, Thomas Greenwood Riley, John Houlker, John Taylor, James Ray, James Whalley, Wm. Banks, Joseph Redhead, James Clayton, and James McDermot. The men agreed to subscribe a penny per week to form a fund out of which a dinner should be provided, and they expressed themselves confident that they could secure the gratuitous services of a band of music. During the meeting there was great order. At the conclusion, a vote of thanks was accorded to the chairman, to the labour master for granting them three-quarters of an hour for the purpose of holding the meeting, and to William Gillow for drawing up the resolutions. Three times three then followed; after which, George Dewhurst mounted a hillock, and, by desire, sang 'Rule Britannia,' the chorus being taken up by the whole crowd, and the whole being wound up with a hearty cheer." There are various schemes devised in Preston for regaling the poor during the guild; and not the worst of them is the proposal to give them a little extra money for that week, so as to enable them to enjoy the holiday with their families at home.

It was now about half-past eleven. "It's getting on for dinner time," said Jackson, looking at his watch. "Let's have a look at th' opposite side yonder; an' then we'll come back, an' you'll see th' men drop work when the five minutes' bell rings. There's many of 'em live so far off that they couldn't well get whoam an' back in an hour; so, we give'em an hour an' a half to their dinner, now, an' they work half an' hour longer i'th afternoon." We crossed the hollow which divides the moor, and went to the top of a sandy cutting at the rear of the workhouse. This eminence commanded a full view of the men at work on different parts of the ground, with the time-keepers going to and fro amongst them, book in hand. Here were men at work with picks and spades; there, a slow-moving train of full barrows came along; and, yonder, a train of empty barrows stood, with the men sitting upon them, waiting. Jackson pointed out some of his most remarkable men to me; after which we went up to a little plot of ground behind the workhouse, where we found a few apparently older or weaker men, riddling pebbly stuff, brought from the bed of the Ribble. The smaller pebbles were thrown into heaps, to make a hard floor for the workhouse schoolyard. The master of the workhouse said that the others were too big for this purpose--the lads would break the windows with them. The largest pebbles were cast aside to be broken up, for the making of garden walks. Whilst the master of the workhouse was showing us round the building, Jackson looked at his watch again, and said, "Come, we've just time to get across again. Th' bell will ring in two or three minutes, an' I should like yo to see 'em knock off." We hurried over to the other side, and, before we had been a minute there, the bell rung. At the first toll, down dropt the barrows, the half-flung shovelfuls fell to the ground, and all labour stopt as suddenly as if the men had been moved by the pull of one string. In two minutes Preston Moor was nearly deserted, and, like the rest, we were on our way to dinner.

CHAPTER XV.

AMONG THE WIGAN OPERATIVES

"There'll be some on us missin', aw deawt, Iv there isn't some help for us soon." --SAMUEL LAYCOCK.

The next scene of my observations is the town of Wigan. The temporary troubles now affecting the working people of Lancashire wear a different aspect there on account of such a large proportion of the population being employed in the coal mines. The "way of life" and the characteristics of the people are marked by strong peculiarities. But, apart from these things, Wigan is an interesting place. The towns of Lancashire have undergone so much change during the last fifty years that their old features are mostly either swept away entirely, or are drowned in a great overgrowth of modern buildings. Yet coaly Wigan retains visible relics of its ancient character still; and there is something striking in its situation. It is associated with some of the most stirring events of our history, and it is the scene of many an interesting old story, such as the legend of Mabel of Haigh Hall, the crusader's dame. The remnant of "Mab's Cross" still stands in Wigan Lane. Some of the finest old halls of Lancashire are now, and have been, in its neighbourhood, such as Ince Hall and Crooke Hall. It must have been a picturesque town in the time of the Commonwealth, when Cavaliers and Roundheads met there in deadly contention. Wigan saw a great deal of the troubles of that time. The ancient monument, erected to the memory of Colonel Tyldesley, upon the ground where he fell at the battle of Wigan Lane, only tells a little of the story of Longfellow's puritan hero, Miles Standish, who belonged to the Chorley branch of the family of Standish of Standish, near this town. The ingenious John Roby, author of the "Traditions of Lancashire," was born here. Round about the old market-place, and the fine parish church of St Wilfred, there are many quaint nooks still left to tell the tale of centuries gone by. These remarks, however, by the way. It is almost impossible to sunder any place entirely from the interest which such things lend to it.

Our present business is with the share which Wigan feels of the troubles of our own time, and in this respect it is affected by some conditions peculiar to the place. I am told that Wigan was one of the first--if not the very first--of the towns of Lancashire to feel the nip of our present distress. I am told, also, that it was the first town in which a Relief Committee was organised. The cotton consumed here is almost entirely of the kind from ordinary to middling American, which is now the scarcest and dearest of any. Preston is almost wholly a spinning town. In Wigan there is a considerable amount of weaving as well as spinning. The counts spun in Wigan are lower than those in Preston; they range from 10's up to 20's. There is also, as I have said before, another peculiar element of labour, which tends to give a strong flavour to the conditions of life in Wigan, that is, the great number of people employed in the coal mines. This, however, does not much lighten the distress which has fallen upon the spinners and weavers, for the colliers are also working short time--an average of four days a week. I am told, also, that the coal miners have been subject to so many disasters of various kinds during past years, that there is now hardly a collier's family which has not lost one or more of its most active members by accidents in the pits. About six years ago, the river Douglas broke into one of the Ince mines, and nearly two hundred people were drowned thereby. These were almost all buried on one day, and it was a very distressing scene. Everywhere in Wigan one may meet with the widows and orphans of men who have been killed in the mines; and there are no few men more or less disabled by colliery accidents, and, therefore, dependent either upon the kindness of their employers, or upon the labour of their families in the cotton factories. This last failing them, the result may be easily guessed. The widows and orphans of coal miners almost always fall back upon factory labour for a living; and, in the present state of things, this class of people forms a very helpless element of the general distress. These things I learnt during my brief visit to the town a few days ago. Hereafter, I shall try to acquaint myself more deeply and widely with the relations of life amongst the working people there.

I had not seen Wigan during many years before that fine August afternoon. In the Main Street and Market Place there is no striking outward sign of distress, and yet here, as in other Lancashire towns, any careful eye may see that there is a visible increase of mendicant stragglers, whose awkward plaintiveness, whose helpless restraint and hesitancy of manner, and whose general appearance, tell at once that they belong to the operative classes now suffering in Lancashire. Beyond this, the sights I first noticed upon the streets, as peculiar to the place, were, here, two "Sisters of Mercy," wending along, in their black cloaks and hoods, with their foreheads and cheeks swathed in ghastly white bands, and with strong rough shoes upon their feet; and, there, passed by a knot of the women employed in the coal mines. The singular appearance of these women has puzzled many a southern stranger. All grimed with coaldust, they swing along the street with their dinner baskets and cans in their hands, chattering merrily. To the waist they are dressed like men, in strong trousers and wooden clogs. Their gowns, tucked clean up, before, to the middle, hang down behind them in a peaked tail. A limp bonnet, tied under the chin, makes up the head-dress. Their curious garb, though soiled, is almost always sound; and one can see that the wash-tub will reveal many a comely face amongst them. The dusky damsels are "to the manner born," and as they walk about the streets, thoughtless of singularity, the Wigan people let them go unheeded by. Before I had been two hours in the town, I was put into communication with one of the active members of the Relief Committee, who offered to devote a few hours of the following day to visitation with me, amongst the poor of a district called "Scholes," on the eastern edge of the town. Scholes is the "Little Ireland" of Wigan, the poorest quarter of the town. The colliers and factory operatives chiefly live there. There is a saying in Wigan --that, no man's education is finished until he has been through Scholes. Having made my arrangements for the next day, I went to stay for the night with a friend who lives in the green country near Orrell, three miles west of Wigan.

Early next morning, we rode over to see the quaint town of Upholland, and its fine old church, with the little ivied monastic ruin close by. We returned thence, by way of "Orrell Pow," to Wigan, to meet my engagement at ten in the forenoon. On our way, we could not help noticing the unusual number of foot-sore, travel-soiled people, many of them evidently factory operatives, limping away from the town upon their melancholy wanderings. We could see, also, by the number of decrepid old women, creeping towards Wigan, and now and then stopping to rest by the wayside, that it was relief day at the Board of Guardians. At ten, I met the gentleman who had kindly offered to guide me for the day; and we set off together. There are three excellent rooms engaged by the good people of Wigan for the employment and teaching of the young women thrown out of work at the cotton mills. The most central of the three is the lecture theatre of the Mechanics' Institution. This room was the first place we visited. Ten o'clock is the time appointed for the young women to assemble. It was a few minutes past ten when we got to the place; and there were some twenty of the girls waiting about the door. They were barred out, on account of being behind time. The lasses seemed very anxious to get in; but they were kept there a few minutes till the kind old superintendent, Mr Fisher, made his appearance. After giving the foolish virgins a gentle lecture upon the value of punctuality, he admitted them to the room. Inside, there were about three hundred and fifty girls mustered that morning. They are required to attend four hours a day on four days of the week, and they are paid 9d. a day for their attendance. They are divided into classes, each class being watched over by some lady of the committee. Part of the time each day is set apart for reading and writing; the rest of the day is devoted to knitting and plain sewing. The business of each day begins with the reading of the rules, after which, the names are called over. A girl in a white pinafore, upon the platform, was calling over the names when we entered. I never saw a more comely, clean, and orderly assembly anywhere. I never saw more modest demeanour, nor a greater proportion of healthy, intelligent faces in any company of equal numbers.

CHAPTER XVI.

"Hopdance cries in Tom's belly for two white herrings. Croak not, black angel; I have no food for thee." --King Lear.

I lingered a little while in the work-room, at the Mechanics' Institution, interested in the scene. A stout young woman came in at a side door, and hurried up to the centre of the room with a great roll of coarse gray cloth, and lin check, to be cut up for the stitchers. One or two of the classes were busy with books and slates; the remainder of the girls were sewing and knitting; and the ladies of the committee were moving about, each in quiet superintendence of her own class. The room was comfortably full, even on the platform; but there was very little noise, and no disorder at all. I say again that I never saw a more comely, clean, and well conducted assembly than this of three hundred and fifty factory lasses. I was told, however, that even these girls show a kind of pride of caste amongst one another. The human heart is much the same in all conditions of life. I did not stay long enough to be able to say more about this place; but one of the most active and intelligent ladies connected with the management said to me afterwards, "Your wealthy manufacturers and merchants must leave a great deal of common stuff lying in their warehouses, and perhaps not very saleable just now, which would be much more valuable to us here than ever it will be to them. Do you think they would like to give us a little of it if we were to ask them nicely?" I said I thought there were many of them who would do so; and I think I said right.

After a little talk with the benevolent old superintendent, whose heart, I am sure, is devoted to the business for the sake of the good it will do, and the evil it will prevent, I set off with my friend to see some of the poor folk who live in the quarter called "Scholes." It is not more than five hundred yards from the Mechanics' Institution to Scholes Bridge, which crosses the little river Douglas, down in a valley in the eastern part of the town. As soon as we were at the other end of the bridge, we turned off at the right hand corner into a street of the poorest sort--a narrow old street, called "Amy Lane." A few yards on the street we came to a few steps, which led up, on the right hand side, to a little terrace of poor cottages, overlooking the river Douglas. We called at one of these cottages. Though rather disorderly just then, it was not an uncomfortable place. It was evidently looked after by some homely dame. A clean old cat dosed upon a chair by the fireside. The bits of cottage furniture, though cheap, and well worn, were all there; and the simple household gods, in the shape of pictures and ornaments, were in their places still. A hardy-looking, brown-faced man, with close-cropped black hair, and a mild countenance, sat on a table by the window, making artificial flies, for fishing. In the corner over his head a cheap, dingy picture of the trial of Queen Catherine, hung against the wall. I could just make out the tall figure of the indignant queen, in the well-known theatrical attitude, with her right arm uplifted, and her sad, proud face turned away from the judgment-seat, where Henry sits, evidently uncomfortable in mind, as she gushes forth that bold address to her priestly foes and accusers. The man sitting beneath the picture, told us that he was a throstle-overlooker by trade; and that he had been nine months out of work. He said, "There's five on us here when we're i'th heawse. When th' wark fell off I had a bit o' brass save't up, so we were forced to start o' usin' that. But month after month went by, an' th' brass kept gettin' less, do what we would; an' th' times geet wur, till at last we fund ersels fair stagged up. At after that, my mother helped us as weel as hoo could,--why, hoo does neaw, for th' matter o' that, an' then aw've three brothers, colliers; they've done their best to poo us through. But they're nobbut wortchin' four days a week, neaw; besides they'n enough to do for their own. Aw make no acceawnt o' slotchin' up an' deawn o' this shap, like a foo. It would sicken a dog, it would for sure. Aw go a fishin' a bit neaw an' then; an' aw cotter abeawt wi' first one thing an' then another; but it comes to no sense. Its noan like gradely wark. It makes me maunder up an' deawn, like a gonnor wi' a nail in it's yed. Aw wish to God yon chaps in Amerikey would play th' upstroke, an' get done wi' their bother, so as folk could start o' their wark again." This was evidently a provident man, who had striven hard to get through his troubles decently. His position as overlooker, too, made him dislike the thoughts of receiving relief amongst the operatives whom he might some day be called upon to superintend again.

A little higher up in Amy Lane we came to a kind of square. On the side where the lane continues there is a dead brick wall; on the other side, bounding a little space of unpaved ground, rather higher than the lane, there are a few old brick cottages, of very mean and dirty appearance. At the doors of some of the cottages squalid, untidy women were lounging; some of them sitting upon the doorstep, with their elbows on their knees, smoking, and looking stolidly miserable. We were now getting near where the cholera made such havoc during its last visit,--a pestilent jungle, where disease is always prowling about, "seeking whom it can devour." A few sallow, dirty children were playing listlessly about the space, in a melancholy way, looking as if their young minds were already "sicklied o'er with the pale cast of thought," and unconsciously oppressed with wonder why they should be born to such a miserable share of human life as this. A tall, gaunt woman, with pale face, and thinly clad in a worn and much-patched calico gown, and with a pair of "trashes" upon her stockingless feet, sat on the step of the cottage nearest the lane. The woman rose when she saw my friend. "Come in," said she; and we followed her into the house. It was a wretched place; and the smell inside was sickly. I should think a broker would not give half-a-crown for all the furniture we saw. The woman seemed simple-minded and very illiterate; and as she stood in the middle of the floor, looking vaguely round she said, "Aw can hardly ax yo to sit deawn, for we'n sowd o' th' things eawt o'th heawse for a bit o' meight; but there is a cheer theer, sich as it is; see yo; tak' that." When she found that I wished to know something of her condition--although this was already well known to the gentleman who accompanied me--she began to tell her story in a simple, off-hand way. "Aw've had nine childer," said she; "we'n buried six, an' we'n three alive, an' aw expect another every day." In one corner there was a rickety little low bedstead. There was no bedding upon it but a ragged kind of quilt, which covered the ticking. Upon this quilt something lay, like a bundle of rags, covered with a dirty cloth. "There's one o' th' childer, lies here, ill," said she. "It's getten' th' worm fayver." When she uncovered that little emaciated face, the sick child gazed at me with wild, burning eyes, and began to whine pitifully. "Husht, my love," said the poor woman; "he'll not hurt tho'! Husht, now; he's noan beawn to touch tho'! He's noan o'th doctor, love. Come, neaw, husht; that's a good lass!" I gave the little thing a penny, and one way and another we soothed her fears, and she became silent; but the child still gazed at me with wild eyes, and the forecast of death on its thin face. The mother began again, "Eh, that little thing has suffered summat," said she, wiping her eyes; "an', as aw towd yo before, aw expect another every day. They're born nake't, an' th' next'll ha' to remain so, for aught that aw con see. But, aw dar not begin o' thinkin' abeawt it. It would drive me crazy. We han a little lad o' mi sister's livin' wi' us. Aw had to tak' him when his mother deed. Th' little thing's noather feyther nor mother, neaw. It's gwon eawt a beggin' this morning wi' my two childer. My mother lives with us, too,"

101

continued she; "hoo's gooin' i' eighty-four, an' hoo's eighteen pence a week off th' teawn. There's seven on us, o'together, an' we'n had eawr share o' trouble, one way an' another, or else aw'm chetted. Well, aw'll tell yo' what happened to my husban' o' i' two years' time. My husban's a collier. Well, first he wur brought whoam wi' three ribs broken--aw wur lyin' in when they brought him whoam. An' then, at after that, he geet his arm broken; an' soon after he'd getten o'er that, he wur nearly brunt to deeath i' one o'th pits at Ratcliffe; an' aw haven't quite done yet, for, after that, he lee ill o'th rheumatic fayver sixteen week. That o' happen't i' two years' time. It's God's truth, maister. Mr Lea knows summat abeawt it--an' he stons theer. Yo may have a like aim what we'n had to go through. An' that wur when times were'n good; but then, everything o' that sort helps to poo folk deawn, yo known. We'n had very hard deed, maister--aw consider we'n had as hard deed as anybody livin', takkin' o' together." This case was an instance of the peculiar troubles to which colliers and their families are liable; a little representative bit of life among the poor of Wigan. From this place we went further up into Scholes, to a dirty square, called the "Coal Yard." Here we called at the house of Peter Y_, a man of fifty-one, and a weaver of a kind of stuff called, "broad cross-over," at which work he earned about six shillings a week, when in full employ. His wife was a cripple, unable to help herself; and, therefore, necessarily a burden. Their children were two girls, and one boy. The old woman said, "Aw'm always forced to keep one o'th lasses a-whoam, for aw connot do a hond's turn." The children had been brought up to factory labour; but both they and their father had been out of work nearly twelve months. During that time the family had received relief tickets, amounting to the value of four shillings a week. Speaking of the old man, the mother said, "Peter has just getten a bit o' work again, thank God. He's hardly fit for it; but he'll do it as lung as he can keep ov his feet."

CHAPTER XVII.

*"Lord! how the people suffer day by day A lingering death, through lack of honest bread; And yet are gentle on their starving way, By faith in future good and justice led." --
BLACKBURN BARD.*

It is a curious thing to note the various combinations of circumstance which exist among the families of the poor. On the surface they seem much the same; and they are reckoned up according to number, income, and the like. But there are great differences of feeling and cultivation amongst them; and then, every household has a story of its own, which no statistics can tell. There is hardly a family which has not had some sickness, some stroke of disaster, some peculiar sorrow, or crippling hindrance, arising within itself, which makes its condition unlike the rest. In this respect each family is one string in the great harp of humanity--a string which, touched by the finger of Heaven, contributes a special utterance to that universal harmony which is too fine for mortal ears.

From the old weaver's house in "Coal Yard" we went to a place close by, called "Castle Yard," one of the most unwholesome nooks I have seen in Wigan yet, though there are many such in that part of the town. It was a close, pestilent, little cul de sac, shut in by a dead brick wall at the far end. Here we called upon an Irish family, seven in number. The mother and two of her daughters were in. The mother had sore eyes. The place was dirty, and the air inside was close and foul. The miserable bits of furniture left were fit for nothing but a bonfire. "Good morning, Mrs K_," said my friend, as we entered the stifling house; "how are you geting on?" The mother stood in the middle of the floor, wiping her sore eyes, and then folding her hands in a tattered apron; whilst her daughters gazed upon us vacantly from the background. "Oh, then," replied the woman, "things is worse wid us entirely, sir, than whenever ye wor here before. I dunno what will we do whin the winter comes." In reply to me, she said, "We are seven altogether, wid my husband an' myself. I have one lad was ill o' the yallow jaundice this many months, an' there is somethin' quare hangin' over that boy this day; I dunno whatever shall we do wid him. I was thinkin' this long time could I get a ricommind to see would the doctor give him anythin' to rise an appetite in him at all. By the same token, I know it is not a convanient time for makin' appetites in poor folk just now. But perhaps the doctor might be able to do him some good, by the way he would be ready when times mind. Faith, my hands is full wid one thing an' another. Ah, thin; but God is good, after all. We dunno what is He goin' to do through the dark stroke is an' us this day." Here my friend interrupted her, saying, "Don't you think, Mrs K_, that you would be more comfortable if you were to keep your house cleaner? It costs nothing, you know, but a little labour; and you have nothing else to do just now." "Ah, then," replied she; "see here, now. I was just gettin' the mug ready for that same, whenever ye wor comin' into the yard, I was. "Here she turned sharply round, and said to one of the girls, who was standing in the background, "Go on, wid ye, now; and clane the flure. Didn't I tell ye many a time this day?" The girl smiled, and shuffled away into a dingy little room at the rear of the cottage. "Faith, sir," continued the woman, beating time with her hand in the air; "faith, sir, it is not aisy for a poor woman to manage unbiddable childer." "What part of Ireland do you come from, Mrs K_?" said I. She hesitated a second or two, and played with her chin; then, blushing slightly, she replied in a subdued tone, "County Galway, sir." "Well," said I, "you've no need to be ashamed of that." The woman seemed reassured, and answered at once, "Oh, indeed then, sir, I am not ashamed--why would I? I am more nor seventeen year now in England, an' I never disguised my speech, nor disowned my country--nor I never will, aither, plase God." She had said before that her husband was forty- five years of age; and now I inquired what age she was. "I am the same age as my husband," replied she. "Forty-five," said I. "No, indeed, I am not forty-five," answered she; "nor forty naither." "Are you thirty-eight?" "May be I am; I dunno. I don't think I am thirty-eight naither; I am the same age as my husband." It was no use talking, so the subject was dropped. As we came away, the woman followed my friend to the door, earnestly pleading the cause of some family in the neighbourhood, who were in great distress. "See now," said she, "they are a large family, and the poor crayters are starvin'. He is a shoemaker, an' he doesn't be gettin' any work this longtime. Oh, indeed, then, Mr Lea, God knows thim people is badly off." My friend promised to visit the family she had spoken of, and we came away. The smell of the house, and of the court altogether, was so sickening that we were glad to get into the air of the open street again.

It was now about half-past eleven, and my friend said, "We have another workroom for young women in the schoolroom of St Catherine's Church. It is about five minutes' walk from here; we have just time to see it before they break up for dinner." It was a large, square, brick building, standing by the road side, upon high ground, at the upper end of Scholes. The church is about fifty yards east of the schoolhouse. This workroom was more airy, and better lighted than the one at the Mechanics' Institution. The floor was flagged, which will make it colder than the other in winter time. There were four hundred girls in this room, some engaged in sewing and knitting, others in reading and writing. They are employed four days in the week, and they are paid ninepence a day, as at the other two rooms in the town. It really was a pleasant thing to see their clear, healthy, blond complexions; their clothing, so clean and whole, however poor; and their orderly deportment. But they had been accustomed to work, and their work had given them a discipline which is not sufficiently valued. There are people who have written a great deal, and know very little about the influence of factory labour upon health,--it would be worth their while to see some of these workrooms. I think it would sweep cobwebs away from the corners of their minds. The clothing made up in these workrooms is of a kind suitable for the wear of working people, and is intended to be given away to the neediest among them, in the coming winter. I noticed a feature here which escaped me in the room at the Mechanics' Institution. On one side of the room there was a flight of wooden stairs, about six yards wide. Upon these steps were seated a number of children, with books in their hands. These youngsters were evidently restless, though not noisy; and they were not very attentive to their books. These children were the worst clad and least clean part of the assembly; and it was natural that they should be so, for they were habitual beggars, gathered from the streets, and brought there to be taught and fed. When they were pointed out to me, I could not help thinking that the money which has been spent upon ragged schools is an excellent investment in the sense of world-wide good. I remarked to one of the ladies teaching there, how very clean and healthy the young women looked. She said that the girls had lately been more in the open air than usual. "And," said she, speaking of the class she was superintending, "I find these poor girls as apt learners as any other class of young people I ever knew." We left the room just before they were dismissed to dinner.

A few yards from the school, and by the same roadside, we came to a little cottage at the end of a row. "We will call here," said my friend; "I know the people very well. "A little, tidy, good-looking woman sat by the fire, nursing an infant at the breast. The house was clean, and all the humble furniture of the poor man's cottage seemed to be still in its place. There were two shelves of books hanging against the walls, and a pile of tracts and pamphlets, a foot deep, on a small table at the back of the room. I soon found, however, that these people were going through their share of the prevalent suffering. The family was six in number. The comely little woman said that her husband was a weaver of "Cross-over;" and I suppose he would earn about six or seven shillings a week at that kind of work; but he had been long out of work. His wife said, "I've had to pop my husban's trousers an' waistcoat many a time to pay th' rent o' this house." She then began to talk about her first-born, and the theme was too much for her. "My owdest child was thirteen when he died," said she. "Eh, he was a fine child. We lost him about two years sin'. He was killed. He fell down that little pit o' Wright's, Mr Lea, he did." Then the little woman began to cry, "Eh, my poor lad! Eh, my fine little lad! Oh dear,--oh dear o' me!" What better thing could we have done than to say nothing at such a moment. We waited a few minutes until she became calm, and then she began to talk about a benevolent young governess who used to live in that quarter, and who had gone about doing good there, amongst "all sorts and conditions of men," especially the poorest.

"Eh," said she; "that was a good woman, if ever there was one. Hoo teached a class o' fifty at church school here, though hoo wur a Dissenter. An' hoo used to come to this house every Sunday neet, an' read th' Scripturs; an' th' place wur olez crammed--th' stairs an o'. Up-groon fellows used to come an' larn fro her, just same as childer--they did for sure--great rough colliers, an' o' mak's. Hoo used to warn 'em again drinkin', an' get 'em to promise that they wouldn't taste for sich a time. An' if ever they broke their promise, they olez towd her th' truth, and owned to it at once. They like as iv they couldn't for shame tell her a lie. There's one of her scholars, a blacksmith--he's above fifty year owd--iv yo were to mention her name to him just now, he'd begin a-cryin', an' he'd ha' to walk eawt o'th heause afore he could sattle hissel'. Eh, hoo wur a fine woman; an' everything that hoo said wur so striking. Hoo writes to her scholars here, once a week; an' hoo wants 'em to write back to her, as mony on 'em as con do. See yo; that's one ov her letters!"

CHAPTER XVIII.

"Come, child of misfortune, come hither! I'll weep with thee, tear for tear." --TOM MOORE.

The weaver's wife spoke very feelingly of the young governess who had been so good to the family. Her voice trembled with emotion as she told of her kindnesses, which had so won the hearts of the poor folk thereabouts, that whenever they hear her name now, their tongues leap at once into heart-warm praise of her. It seems to have been her daily pleasure to go about helping those who needed help most, without any narrowness of distinction; in the spirit of that "prime wisdom" which works with all its might among such elements as lie nearest to the hand. Children and gray-haired working men crowded into the poor cottages to hear her read, and to learn the first elements of education at her free classes. She left the town, some time ago, to live in the south of England; but the blessings of many who were ready to perish in Wigan will follow her all her days, and her memory will long remain a garden of good thoughts and feelings to those she has left behind. The eyes of the weaver's wife grew moist as she told of the old blacksmith, who could not bear to hear her name mentioned without tears. On certain nights of the week he used to come regularly with the rest to learn to read, like a little child, from that young teacher. As I said in my last, she still sends a weekly letter to her poor scholars in Wigan to encourage them in their struggles, and to induce as many of them as are able to write to her in return. "This is one of her letters," said the poor woman, handing a paper to me. The manner of the handwriting was itself characteristic of kind consideration for her untrained readers. The words stood well apart. The letters were clearly divided, and carefully and distinctly written, in Roman characters, a quarter of an inch long; and there was about three-quarters of an inch of space between each line, so as to make the whole easier to read by those not used to manuscript. The letter ran as follows:--"Dear friends,--I send you with this some little books, which I hope you will like to try to read; soon, I hope, I shall be able to help you with those texts you cannot make out by yourselves. I often think of you, dear friends, and wish that I could sometimes take a walk to Scholefield's Lane. This wish only makes me feel how far I am from you, but then I remember with gladness that I may mention you all by name to our one Father, and ask Him to bless you. Very often I do ask Him, and one of my strongest wishes is that we, who have so often read His message of love together, may all of us love the Saviour, and, through Him, be saved from sin. Dear friends, do pray to Him. With kind love and best wishes to each one of you, believe me always, your sincere friend, __." I have dwelt a little upon this instance of unassuming beneficence, to show that there is a great deal of good being done in this world, which is not much heard of, except by accident. One meets with it, here and there, as a thirsty traveller meets with an unexpected spring in the wilderness, refreshing its own plot of earth, without noise or ostentation.

My friend and I left the weaver's cottage, and came down again into a part of Scholes where huddled squalor and filth is to be found on all sides. On our way we passed an old tattered Irishwoman, who was hurrying along, with two large cabbages clipt tight in her withered arms. "You're doin' well, old lady," said I. "Faith," replied she, "if I had a big lump ov a ham bone, now, wouldn't we get over this day in glory, anyhow. But no matter. There's not wan lafe o' them two fellows but will be clane out o' sight before the clock strikes again." The first place we called at in this quarter was a poor half-empty cottage, inhabited by an old widow and her sick daughter. The girl sat there pale and panting, and wearing away to skin and bone. She was far gone in consumption. Their only source of maintenance was the usual grant of relief from the committee, but this girl's condition needed further consideration. The old widow said to my friend, "Aw wish yo could get me some sort o' nourishment for this lass, Mr Lea; aw cannot get it mysel', an' yo see'n heaw hoo is." My friend took a note of the case, and promised to see to it at once. When great weltering populations, like that of Lancashire, are thrown suddenly into such a helpless state as now, it is almost impossible to lay hold at once of every nice distinction of circumstances that gives a speciality of suffering to the different households of the poor. But I believe, as this time of trouble goes on, the relief committees are giving a more careful and delicate consideration to the respective conditions of poor families.

After leaving the old widow's house, as we went farther down into the sickly hive of penury and dirt, called "Scholes," my friend told me of an intelligent young woman, a factory operative and a Sunday-school teacher, who had struggled against starvation, till she could bear it no longer; and, even after she had accepted the grant of relief, she "couldn't for shame" fetch the tickets herself, but waited outside whilst a friend of hers went in for them. The next house we visited was a comfortable cottage. The simple furniture was abundant, and good of its kind, and the whole was remarkably clean. Amongst the wretched dwellings in its neighbourhood, it shone "like a good deed in a naughty world." On the walls there were several Catholic pictures, neatly framed; and a large old-fashioned wooden wheel stood in the middle of the floor, with a quantity of linen yarn upon it. Old Stephen I__ and his cosy goodwife lived there. The old woman was "putting the place to rights" after their noontide meal; and Stephen was "cottering" about the head of the cellar steps when we went in. There were a few healthy plants in the windows, and everything gave evidence of industry and care. The good-tempered old couple were very communicative. Old Stephen was a weaver of diaper; and, when he had anything to do, he could earn about eight shillings a week. "Some can get more than that at the same work," said he; "but I am gettin' an old man, ye see. I shall be seventy-three on the 10th of next October, and, beside that, I have a very bad arm, which is a great hindrance to me." "He has had very little work for months, now," said his wife; "an' what makes us feel it more, just now, is that my son is over here on a visit to us, from Oscott College. He is studying for the priesthood. He went to St John's, here, in Wigan, for five years, as a pupil teacher; an' he took good ways, so the principals of the college proposed to educate him for the Church of Rome. He was always a good boy, an' a bright one, too. I wish we had been able to entertain him better. But he knows that the times are again us. He is twenty-four years of age; an' I often think it strange that his father's birthday and his own fall on the same day of the month-- the 10th of October. I hope we'll both live to see him an ornament to his profession yet. There is only the girl, an' Stephen, an' myself left at home now, an' we have hard work to pull through, I can assure ye; though there are many people a dale worse off than we are."

From this place we went up to a street called "Vauxhall Road." In the first cottage we called at here the inmates were all out of work, as usual, and living upon relief. There happened to be a poor old white-haired weaver sitting in the house,--an aged neighbour out of work, who had come in to chat with my friend a bit. My friend asked how he was getting on. "Yo mun speak up," said the woman of the house, "he's very deaf." "What age are yo, maister?" said I. "What?" "How old are yo?" "Aw'm a beamer," replied the old man, "a twister-in,--when there's ought doin'. But it's nowt ov a trade neaw. Aw'll tell yo what ruins me; it's these

113

lung warps. They maken 'em seven an' eight cuts in, neaw an' then. There's so mony 'fancies' an' things i' these days; it makes my job good to nought at o' for sich like chaps as me. When one gets sixty year owd, they needen to go to schoo again neaw; they getten o'erta'en wi' so many kerly-berlies o' one mak and another. Mon, owd folk at has to wortch for a livin' cannot keep up wi' sich times as these,--nought o'th sort." "Well, but how do you manage to live?" "Well, aw can hardly tell,--aw'll be sunken iv aw can tell. It's very thin pikein'; but very little does for me, an' aw've nought but mysel'. Yo see'n, aw get a bit ov a job neaw an' then, an' a scrat amung th' rook, like an owd hen. But aw'll tell yo one thing; aw'll not go up yon, iv aw can help it,--aw'll not." ("Up yon" meant to the Board of Guardians.) "Eh, now," said the woman of the house, "aw never see'd sich a man as him i' my life. See yo, he'll sit an' clem fro mornin' to neet afore he'll ax oather relief folk or onybody else for a bite."

In the same street we called at a house where there was a tall, pale old man, sitting sadly in an old arm-chair, by the fireside. The little cottage was very sweet and orderly. Every window was cleaned to its utmost nook of glass, and every bit of metal was brightened up to the height. The flagged floor was new washed; and everything was in its own place. There were a few books on little shelves, and a Bible lay on the window-sill; and there was a sad, chapel-like stillness in the house. A clean, staid-looking girl stood at a table, peeling potatoes for dinner. The old man said, "We are five, altogether, in this house. This lass is a reeler. I am a weighver; but we'n bin out o' wark nine months, now. We'n bin force't to tak to relief at last; an' we'n getten five tickets. We could happen ha' manage't better,--but aw'm sore wi' rheumatism, yo see'n. Aw've had a bit o' weighvin' i'th heawse mony a day, but aw've th' rheumatic so bad i' this hond--it's hond that aw pick wi'--that aw couldn't bide to touch a fither with it, bless yo. Aw have th' rheumatic all o'er mo, nearly; an' it leads one a feaw life. Yo happen never had a touch on it, had yo?" "Never." "Well; yo're weel off. When is this war to end, thinken yo?" "Nay; that's a very hard thing to tell." " Well, we mun grin an' abide till it's o'er, aw guess. It's a mad mak o' wark. But it'll happen turn up for best i'th end ov o'."

CHAPTER XIX.

"Mother, heaw leets we han no brade,-- Heawever con it be? Iv aw don't get some brade to eat, Aw think 'at aw mun dee." --Hungry Child.

It was about noon when we left the old weaver, nursing his rheumatic limbs by the side of a dim fire, in his chapel-like little house. His daughter, a tall, clean, shy girl, began to peel a few potatoes just before we came away. It is a touching thing, just now, to see so many decent cottages of thrifty working men brought low by the strange events of these days; cottages in which everything betokens the care of well-conducted lives, and where the sacred fire of independent feeling is struggling through the long frost of misfortune with patient dignity. It is a touching thing to see the simple joys of life, in homes like these, crushed into a speechless endurance of penury, and the native spirit of self-reliance writhing in unavoidable prostration, and hoping on from day to day for better times. I have seen many such places in my wanderings during these hard days--cottages where all was so sweet and orderly, both in person and habitation, that, but for the funereal stillness which sat upon hunger-nipt faces, a stranger would hardly have dreamt that the people dwelling there were undergoing any uncommon privation. I have often met with such people in my rambles,--I have often found them suffering pangs more keen than hunger alone could inflict, because they arose from the loss of those sweet relations of independence which are dear to many of them as life itself. With such as these--the shy, the proud, the intelligent and uncomplaining endurers--hunger is not the hardest thing that befalls:-

"When the mind's free, The body's delicate; the tempest in their minds Doth from their senses take all else, Save what beats there."

People of this temper are more numerous amongst our working population than the world believes, because they are exactly of the kind least likely to be heard of. They will fight their share of the battle of this time out as nobly as they have begun it; and it will be an ill thing for the land that owns them if full justice is not done to their worth, both now and hereafter.

In the same street where the old weaver lived, we called upon a collier's family--a family of ten in number. The colliers of Wigan have been suffering a good deal lately, among the rest of the community, from shortness of labour. It was dinner-time when we entered the house, and the children were all swarming about the little place clamouring for their noontide meal. With such a rough young brood, I do not wonder that the house was not so tidy as some that I had seen. The collier's wife was a decent, good-tempered- looking woman, though her face was pale and worn, and bore evidence of the truth of her words, when she said, "Bless your life, aw'm poo'd to pieces wi' these childer!" She sat upon a stool, nursing a child at the breast, and doing her best to still the tumult of the others, who were fluttering about noisily. "Neaw, Sammul," said she, "theaw'll ha' that pot upo th' floor in now,--thae little pousement thae! Do keep eawt o' mischief,--an' make a less din, childer, win yo:

for my yed's fair maddle't wi' one thing an' another . . . Mary, tak' th' pon off th' fire, an' reach me yon hippin' off th' oondur; an' then sit tho deawn somewheer, do,--thae'll be less bi th' legs." The children ranged seemingly from about two months up to fourteen years of age. Two of the youngest were sitting upon the bottom step of the stairs, eating off one plate. Four rough lads were gathered round a brown dish, which stood upon a little deal table in the middle of the floor. These four were round-headed little fellows, all teeming with life. "Yon catched us eawt o'flunters, (out of order,)" said the poor woman when we entered; "but what con a body do?" We were begging that she would not disturb herself, when one of the lads at the table called out, "Mother; look at eawr John. He keeps pushin' me off th' cheer!" "Eh, John," replied she; "I wish thy feyther were here! Thae'rt olez tormentin' that lad. Do let him alone, wilto--or else aw'll poo that toppin' o' thine, smartly--aw will! An' do see iv yo connot behave yorsels!" "Well," said John; "he keeps takkin' my puddin'!" "Eh, what a story," replied the other little fellow; "it wur thee, neaw!" " Aw'll tell yo what it is," said the mother, "iv yo two connot agree, an' get your dinner quietly, aw'll tak that dish away; an' yo'st not have another bite this day. Heaw con yo for shame!" This quietened the lads a little, and they went on with their dinner. At another little table under the back window, two girls stood, dining off one plate. The children were all eating a kind of light pudding, known in Lancashire by the name of "Berm-bo," or, "Berm-dumplin'," made of flour and yeast, mixed with a little suet. The poor woman said that her children were all "hearty-etten," (all hearty eaters,) especially the lads; and she hardly knew what to make for them, so as to have enough for the whole. "Berm-dumplin'," was as satisfying as anything that she could get, and it would "stick to their ribs" better than "ony mak o' swill;" besides, the children liked it. Speaking of her husband, she said, "He were eawt o' wark a good while; but he geet a shop at last, at Blackrod, abeawt four mile off Wigan. When he went a-wortchin' to Blackrod, at first, nought would sarve but he would walk theer an' back every day, so as to save lodgin' brass,--an sich like. Aw shouldn't ha' care't iv it had nobbut bin a mile, or two even; for aw'd far rayther that he had his meals comfortable awhoam, an' his bits o' clooas put reet; but Lord bless yo,--eight mile a day, beside a hard day's wark,--it knocked him up at last,--it were so like. He kept sayin', 'Oh, he could do it,' an' sich like; but aw could see that he were fair killin' hissel', just for the sake o' comin' to his own whoam ov a neet; an' for th' sake o' savin' two or three shillin'; so at last aw turned Turk, an' made him tak lodgin's theer. Aw'd summut to do to persuade him at first, an' aw know that he's as whoam-sick as a chylt that's lost its mother, just this minute; but then, what's th' matter o' that,--it wouldn't do for mo to have him laid up, yo known. . . . Oh, he's a very feelin' mon. Aw've sin him when he couldn't finish his bit o' dinner for thinkin' o' somebody that were clemmin'." Speaking of the hardships the family had experienced, she said, "Eh, bless yo! There's some folk can sit i'th heawse an' send their childer to prow eawt a-beggin' in a mornin', regilar,--but eawr childer wouldn't do it,--an', iv they would, aw wouldn' let 'em,-- naw, not iv we were clemmin' to deeoth,--to my thinkin'."

The woman was quite right. Among the hard-tried operatives of Lancashire I have seen several instances in which they have gone out daily to beg; and some rare cases, even, in which they have stayed moodily at home themselves and sent their children forth to beg; and anybody living in this county will have noticed the increase of mendicancy there, during the last few months. No doubt professional beggars have taken large advantage of this unhappy time to work upon the sympathies of those easy givers who cannot bear to hear the wail of distress, however simulated--who prefer giving at once, because it "does their own hearts good," to the trouble of inquiring or the pain of refusing,--who would rather relieve twenty rogues than miss the blessing of one honest soul who was ready to perish,--those kind-hearted, free-handed scatterers of indiscriminate benevolence who are the keen-eyed, whining cadger's chief support, his standing joke, and favourite prey; and who are more than ever disposed to give to whomsoever shall ask of them in such a season as this. All the mendicancy which appears on our streets does not belong to the suffering operatives of Lancashire. But, apart from those poor, miserable crawlers in the gutters of life, who live by habitual and unnecessary beggary, great and continued adversity is a strong test of the moral tone of any people. Extreme poverty, and the painful things which follow in its train--these are "bad to bide" with the best of mankind. Besides, there are always some people who, from causes within themselves, are continually at their wits' end to keep the wolf from the door, even when employment is plentiful with them; and there are some natures too weak to bear any long strain of unusual poverty without falling back upon means of living which, in easy circumstances, they would have avoided, if not despised. It is one evil of the heavy pressure of the times; for there is fear that among such as these, especially the young and plastic, some may become so familiar with that beggarly element which was offensive to their minds at first--may so lose the tone of independent pride, and become "subdued to what they work in, like the dyer's hand,"--that they may learn to look upon mendicancy as an easy source of support hereafter, even in times of less difficulty than the present.

Happily, such weakness as this is not characteristic of the English people; but "they are well kept that God keeps," and perhaps it would not be wise to cramp the hand of relief too much at a time like this, to a people who have been, and will be yet, the hope and glory of the land.

CHAPTER XX.

"Poor Tom's a-cold! Who gives anything to poor Tom?" -- King Lear.

One sometimes meets with remarkable differences of condition in the households of poor folk, which stand side by side in the same street. I am not speaking of the uncertain shelters of those who struggle upon the skirts of civilisation, in careless, uncared-for wretchedness, without settled homes, or regular occupation,--the miserable camp followers of life's warfare,--living habitually from hand to mouth, in a reckless wrestle with the world, for mere existence. I do not mean these, but the households of our common working people. Amongst the latter one sometimes meets with striking differences, in cleanliness, furniture, manners, intellectual acquirements, and that delicate compound of mental elements called taste. Even in families whose earnings have been equal in the past, and who are just now subject alike to the same pinch of adversity, these disparities are sometimes very great. And, although there are cases in which the immediate causes of these differences are evident enough in the habits of the people, yet, in others, the causes are so obscure, that the wisest observer would be most careful in judging respecting them. I saw an example of this in a little bye-street, at the upper end of Scholes--a quarter of Wigan where the poorest of the poor reside, and where many decent working people have lately been driven for cheap shelter by the stress of the times. Scholes is one of those ash-pits of human life which may be found in almost any great town; where, among a good deal of despised stuff, which by wise treatment might possibly be made useful to the world, many a jewel gets accidentally thrown away, and lost. This bye-street of mean brick cottages had an unwholesome, outcast look; and the sallow, tattered women, lounging about the doorways, and listlessly watching the sickly children in the street, evinced the prevalence of squalor and want there. The very children seemed joyless at their play; and everything that met the eye foretold that there was little chance of finding anything in that street but poverty in its most prostrate forms. But, even in this unpromising spot, I met with an agreeable surprise.

The first house we entered reminded me of those clean, lone dwellings, up in the moorland nooks of Lancashire, where the sweet influences of nature have free play; where the people have a hereditary hatred of dirt and disorder; and where, even now, many of the hardy mountain folk are half farmers, half woollen weavers, doing their weaving in their own quiet houses, where the smell of the heather and the song of the wild bird floats in at the workman's window, blent with the sounds of rindling waters,--doing their weaving in green sequestered nooks, where the low of kine, and the cry of the moorfowl can be heard; and bearing the finished "cuts" home upon their backs to the distant town. All was so bright in this little cottage,--so tidy and serene,--that the very air seemed clearer there than in the open street. The humble furniture, good of its kind, was all shiny with "elbow grease," and some parts of it looked quaint and well-preserved, like the heirlooms of a careful cottage ancestry. The well polished fire-irons, and other metal things, seemed to gather up the diffuse daylight and fling it back in concentrated radiances that illuminated the shady cottage with cheerful beauty. The little shelf of books, the gleaming window, with its healthy pot flowers, the perfect order, and the trim sweetness of everything, reminded me, as I have said, of the better sort of houses where simple livers dwell, up among the free air of the green hills--those green hills of Lancashire, the remembrance of which will always stir my heart as long as it can stir to anything. This cottage, in comparison with most of those which I had seen in Scholes, looked like a glimpse of the star-lit blue peeping through the clouds on a gloomy night. I found that it was the house of a widower, a weaver of diaper, who was left with a family of eight children to look after. Two little girls were in the house, and they were humbly but cleanly clad. One of them called her father up from the cellar, where he was working at his looms. He was a mild, thoughtful-looking man, something past middle age. I could not help admiring him as he stood in the middle of the floor with his unsleeved arms folded, uttering quiet jets of simple speech to my friend, who had known him before. He said that he hardly ever got anything to do now, but when he was at work he could make about 7s. 2d. a week by weaving two cuts. He was receiving six tickets weekly from the Relief Committee, which, except the proceeds of a little employment now and then, was all that the family of nine had to depend upon for food, firing, clothes, and rent. He said that he was forced to make every little spin out as far as it would; but it kept him bare and busy, and held his nose "everlastingly deawn to th' grindlestone." But he didn't know that it was any use complaining about a thing that neither master nor man could help. He durst say that he could manage to grin and bide till things came round, th' same as other folk had to do. Grumbling, in a case like this, was like "fo'in eawt wi' th' elements," (quarrelling with a storm.) One of his little girls was on her knees, cleaning the floor. She stopped a minute, to look at my friend and me. "Come, my lass," said her father, "get on wi' thi weshin'." "I made application for th' watchman's place at Leyland Mill," continued he, "but I wur to lat. . . . There's nought for it," continued he, as we came out of the house, "there's nought for it but to keep one's een oppen, an' do as weel as they con, till it blows o'er."

A few yards from this house, we looked in at a slip of a cottage, at the corner of the row. It was like a slice off some other cottage, stuck on at the end of the rest, to make up the measure of the street; for it was less than two yards wide, by about four yards long. There was only one small window, close to the door, and it was shrouded by a dingy cotton blind. When we first entered, I could hardly see what there was in that gloomy cell; but when the eyes became acquainted with the dimness within, we found that there was neither fire nor furniture in the place, except at the far end, where an old sick woman lay gasping upon three chairs, thinly covered from the cold. She was dying of asthma. At her right hand there was another rickety chair, by the help of which she raised herself up from her hard bed. She said that she had never been up stairs during the previous twelve months, but had lain there, at the foot of the stairs, all that time. She had two daughters. They were both out of the house; and they had been out of work a long time. One of them had gone to Miss B_'s to learn to sew. "She gets her breakfast before she starts," said the old woman, "an' she takes a piece o' bread with her, to last for th' day." It was a trouble to her to talk much, so we did not stop long; but I could not help feeling sorry that the poor old soul had not a little more comfort to smooth her painful passage to the grave. On our way from this place, we went into a cottage near the "Coal Yard," where a tall, thin Irishwoman was washing some tattered clothes, whilst her children played about the gutter outside. This was a family of seven, and they were all out of work, except the father, who was away, trying to make a trifle by hawking writing-paper and envelopes. This woman told us that she was in great trouble about one of her children--the eldest daughter, now grown up to womanhood. "She got married to a sailor about two year ago," said she, "an' he wint away a fortnit after, an' never was heard of since. She never got the scrape ov a pen from him to say was he alive or dead.

She never heard top nor tail of him since he wint from her; an' the girl is just pinin' away."

Poor folk have their full share of the common troubles of life, apart from the present distress. The next place we visited was the "Fleece Yard," another of those unhealthy courts, of which there are so many in Scholes--where poverty and dirt unite to make life doubly miserable. In this yard we went up three or four steps into a little disorderly house, where a family of eleven was crowded. Not one of the eleven was earning anything except the father, who was working for 1s. 3d. a day. In addition to this the family received four tickets weekly from the Relief Committee. There were several of the children in, and they looked brisk and healthy, in spite of the dirt and discomfort of the place; but the mother was sadly "torn down" by the cares of her large family. The house had a sickly smell. Close to the window, a little, stiff built, bullet-headed lad stood, stript to the waist, sputtering and splashing as he washed himself in a large bowl of water, placed upon a stool. By his side there was another lad three or four years older, and the two were having a bit of famous fun together, quite heedless of all else. The elder kept ducking the little fellow's head into the water, upon which the one who was washing himself sobbed, and spat, and cried out in great glee, "Do it again, Jack!" The mother, seeing us laugh at the lads, said, "That big un's been powin' tother, an' th' little monkey's gone an' cut every smite o' th' lad's toppin' off. "" Well," said the elder lad, "Aw did it so as nobody can lug him. "And it certainly was a close clip. We could see to the roots of the little fellow's hair all over his round, hard head. "Come," said the mother, "yo two are makin' a nice floor for mo. Thae'll do, mon; arto beawn to lother o' th' bit o' swoap away that one has to wash wi'; gi's howd on't this minute, an' go thi ways an' dry thisel', thae little pouse, thae." We visited several other places in Scholes that day, but of these I will

125

say something hereafter. In the evening I returned home, and the thing that I best remember hearing on the way was an anecdote of two Lancashire men, who had been disputing a long time about something that one of them knew little of. At last the other turned to him, and said, "Jem; does thae know what it is that makes me like thee so weel, owd brid?" "Naw; what is it?" "Why; it's becose thae'rt sich a ___ foo!" "Well," replied the other, "never thee mind that;" and then, alluding to the subject they had been disputing about, he said, "Thae knows, Joe, aw know thae'rt reet enough; but, by th' men, aw'll not give in till mornin'."

CHAPTER XXI.

*"Here, take this purse, thou whom the Heaven's plagues
Have humbled to all strokes." --King Lear.*

In the afternoon of the last day I spent in Wigan, as I wandered with my friend from one cottage to another, in the long suburban lane called "Hardy Butts," I bethought me how oft I had met with this name of "Butts "connected with places in or close to the towns of Lancashire. To me the original application of the name seems plain, and not uninteresting. In the old days, when archery was common in England, the bowmen of Lancashire were famous; and it is more than likely that these yet so-called "Butts" are the places where archery was then publicly practised. When Sir Edward Stanley led the war-smiths of Lancashire and Cheshire to Flodden Field, the men of Wigan are mentioned as going with the rest. And among those "fellows fearce and freshe for feight," of whom the quaint old alliterative ballad describes the array:-

"A stock of striplings strong of heart, Brought up from babes with beef and bread, From Warton unto Warrington From Wigan unto Wiresdale--"

and, from a long list of the hills, and cloughs, and old towns of the county--the bowmen of Lancashire did their share of work upon that field. The use of the bow lingered longer in Lancashire than in some parts of the kingdom--longer in England generally than many people suppose. Sir Walter Scott says, in a note to his "Legend of Montrose:" "Not only many of the Highlanders in Montrose's army used these antique missiles, but even in England the bow and quiver, once the glory of the bold yeomen of that land, were occasionally used during the great civil wars."

But I have said enough upon this subject in this place. My friend's business, and mine, in Wigan, that day, was connected with other things. He was specially wishful that I should call upon an acquaintance of his, who lived in "Hardy Butts," an old man and very poor; a man heavily stricken by fortune's blows, yet not much tamed thereby; a man "steeped to the lips" in poverty, yet of a jocund spirit; a humorist and a politician, among his humble companions. I felt curious to see this "Old John," of whom I heard so much. We went to the cottage where he lived. There was very little furniture in the place, and, like the house itself, it was neither good nor clean; but then the poverty-stricken pair were very old, and, so far as household comfort went, they had to look after themselves. When we entered, the little wrinkled woman sat with her back to us, smoking, and gazing at the dirty grate, where a few hot cinders glowed dimly in the lowmost bars. "Where's John?" said my friend. "He hasn't bin gone eawt aboon five minutes," said she, turning round to look at us, "Wur yo wantin' him?" "Yes, I should like to see him." She looked hard at my friend again, and then cried out, "Eh, is it yo? Come, an' sit yo deawn! aw'll go an' see iv aw can root him up for yo!" But we thought it as well to visit some other houses in the neighbourhood, calling at old John's again afterwards; so we told the old woman, and came away.

My friend was well known to the poor people of that neighbourhood as a member of the Relief Committee, and we had not gone many yards down "Hardy Butts" before we drew near where three Irishwomen were sitting upon the doorsteps of a miserable cottage, chattering, and looking vacantly up and down the slutchy street. As soon as they caught sight of my friend, one of the women called out, "Eh, here's Mr Lea! Come here, now, Mr Lea, till I spake to ye. Ah, now; couldn't ye do somethin' for old Mary beyant there? Sure the colour of hunger's in that woman's face. Faith, it's a pity to see the way she is,--neither husband nor son, nor chick nor child, nor bit nor sup, barrin' what folk that has nothin' can give to her,--the crayter." " Oh, indeed, then, sir," said another, "I'll lave it to God; but that woman is starvin'. She is little more nor skin an' bone,-- and that's goin' less. Faith, she's not long for this world, any how. . . . Bridget, ye might run an' see can she come here a minute. . . . But there she is, standin' at the corner. Mary! Come here, now, woman, till ye see the gentleman." She was a miserable- looking creature; old, and ill, and thinly-clothed in rags, with a dirty cloth tied round her head. My friend asked her some questions, which she answered slowly, in a low voice that trembled with more than the weakness of old age. He promised to see to the relief of her condition immediately-- and she thanked him, but so feebly, that it seemed to me as if she had not strength enough left to care much whether she was relieved or not.

But, as we came away, the three Irishwomen, sitting upon the door- steps, burst forth into characteristic expressions of gratitude. "Ah! long life to ye, Mr Lea! The prayer o' the poor is wid ye for evermore. If there was ony two people goin' to heaven alive, you'll be wan o' them. . .

That ye may never know want nor scant,--for the good heart that's batein' in ye, Mr Lea." We now went through some of the filthy alleys behind "Hardy Butts," till we came to the cottage of a poor widow and her two daughters. The three were entirely dependent upon the usual grant of relief from the committee. My friend called here to inquire why the two girls had not been to school during the previous few days; and whilst their mother was explaining the reason, a neighbour woman who had seen us enter, looked in at the door, and said, "Hey! aw say, Mr Lea!" "Well, what's the matter?" " Whaw, there's a woman i'th next street at's gettin' four tickets fro th' relief folk, reggilar, an' her husban's addlin' thirty shillin' a week o' t' time, as a sinker--he is for sure. Aw 'm noan tellin' yo a wort ov a lie. Aw consider sick wark as that's noan reet--an' so mony folk clemmin' as there is i' Wigan." He made a note of the matter; but he told me afterwards that such reports were often found to be untrue, having their origin sometimes in private spite or personal contention of some kind.

In the next house we called at, a widow woman lived, with her married daughter, who had a child at the breast. The old woman told her story herself; the daughter never spoke a word, so far as I remember, but sat there, nursing, silent and sad, with half-averted face, and stealing a shy glance at us now and then, when she thought we were not looking at her. It was a clean cottage, though it was scantily furnished with poor things; and they were both neat and clean in person, though their clothing was meagre and far worn. I thought, also, that the old woman's language, and the countenances of both of them, indicated more natural delicacy of feeling, and more cultivation, than is common amongst people of their condition. The old woman said, "My daughter has been eawt o' work a long time. I can make about two shillings and sixpence a-week, an' we've a lodger that pays us two shillings a week; but we've three shillings a-week to pay for rent, an' we must pay it, too, or else turn out. But I'm lookin' for a less heawse; for we cannot afford to stop here any longer, wi' what we have comin' in, --that is, if we're to live at o'." I thought the house they were in was small enough and mean enough for the poorest creature, and, though it was kept clean, the neighbourhood was very unwholesome. But this was another instance of how the unemployed operatives of Lancashire are being driven down from day to day deeper into the pestilent sinks of life in these hard times. "This child of my daughter's," continued the old woman, in a low tone, "this child was born just as they were puttin' my husband into his coffin, an' wi' one thing an' another, we've had a deal o' trouble. But one half o'th world doesn't know how tother lives. My husban' lay ill i' bed three year; an' he suffered to that degree that he was weary o' life long before it were o'er. At after we lost him, these bad times coom on, an' neaw, aw think we're poo'd deawn as nee to th' greawnd as ony body can be. My daughter's husband went off a-seekin' work just afore that child was born,--an' we haven't heard from him yet." My friend took care that his visit should result in lightening the weight of the old woman's troubles a little.

As we passed the doors of a row of new cottages at the top end of "Hardy Butts," a respectable old man looked out at one of the doorways, and said to my friend, "Could aw spake to yo a minute?" We went in, and found the house remarkably clean, with good cottage furniture in it. Two neighbour children were peeping in at the open door. The old man first sent them away, and then, after closing the door, he pointed to a good-looking young woman who stood blushing at the entrance of the inner room, with a wet cloth in her hands, and he said, "Could yo do a bit o' summat to help this lass till sich times as hoo can get wark again? Hoo's noather feyther nor mother, nor nought i'th world to tak to, but what aw can spare for her, an' this is a poor shop to come to for help. Aw'm uncle to her." "Well," said my friend, "and cannot you manage to keep her?" "God bless yo!" replied the old man, getting warm, "Aw cannot keep mysel'. Aw will howd eawt as lung as aw can; but, yo know, what'll barely keep one alive 'll clem two. Aw should be thankful iv yo could give her a bit o' help whol things are as they are." Before the old man had done talking, his niece had crept away into the back room, as if ashamed of being the subject of such a conversation. This case was soon disposed of to the satisfaction of the old man; after which we visited three other houses in the same block, of which I have nothing special to say, except that they were all inhabited by people brought down to destitution by long want of work, and living solely upon the relief fund, and upon the private charity of their old employers. Upon this last source of relief too little has been said, because it has not paraded itself before the public eye; but I have had opportunities for seeing how wide and generous it is, and I shall have abundant occasion for speaking of it hereafter. On our way back, we looked in at "Old John's" again, to see if he had returned home. He had been in, and he had gone out again, so we came away, and saw nothing of him. Farther down towards the town, we passed through Acton Square, which is a cleaner place than some of the abominable nooks of Scholes, though I can well believe that there is many a miserable dwelling in it, from what I saw of the interiors and about the doorways, in passing.

The last house we called at was in this square, and it was a pleasing exception to the general dirt of the neighbourhood. It was the cottage of a stout old collier, who lost his right leg in one of Wright's pits some years ago. My friend knew the family, and we called there more for the purpose of resting ourselves and having a chat than anything else. The old man was gray-haired, but he looked very hale and hearty--save the lack of his leg. His countenance was expressive of intelligence and good humour; and there was a touch of quiet majesty about his massive features. There was, to me, a kind of rude hint of Christopher North in the old collier's appearance. His wife, too, was a tall, strong-built woman, with a comely and a gentle face --a fit mate for such a man as he. I thought, as she moved about, her grand bulk seemed to outface the narrow limits of the cottage. The tiny house was exceedingly clean, and comfortably furnished. Everything seemed to be in its appointed place, even to the sleek cat sleeping on the hearth. There were a few books on a shelf, and a concertina upon a little table in the corner. When we entered, the old collier was busy with the slate and pencil, and an arithmetic before him; but he laid them aside, and, doffing his spectacles, began to talk with us. He said that they were a family of six, and all out of work; but he said that, ever since he lost his leg, the proprietors of the pit in which the accident happened (Wright's) had allowed him a pension of six shillings a week, which he considered very handsome. This allowance just kept the wolf from their little door in these hard times. In the course of our conversation I found that the old man read the papers frequently, and that he was a man of more than common information in his class. I should have been glad to stay longer with him, but my time was up; so I came away from the town, thus ending my last ramble amongst the unemployed operatives of Wigan. Since then the condition of the poor there has been steadily growing worse, which is sure to be heard of in the papers.

CHAPTER XXII.

AN INCIDENT BY THE WAYSIDE.

"Take physic, pomp! Expose thyself to feel what wretches feel; That thou mayst shake the superflux to them, And show the Heavens more just." --King Lear.

On the Saturday after my return from Wigan, a little incident fell in my way, which I thought worth taking note of at the time; and perhaps it may not be uninteresting to your readers. On that day I went up to Levenshulme, to spend the afternoon with an old friend of mine, a man of studious habits, living in a retired part of that green suburb. The time went pleasantly by whilst I was with the calm old student, conversing upon the state of Lancashire, and the strange events which are upheaving the civilised world in great billows of change,--and drinking in the peaceful charm which pervaded everything about the man and his house and the scene which it stood in.

After tea, he came with me across the fields to the "Midway Inn," on Stockport Road, where the omnibuses call on their way to Manchester. It was a lovely evening, very clear and cool, and twilight was sinking upon the scene. Waiting for the next omnibus, we leaned against the long wooden watering-trough in front of the inn. The irregular old building looked picturesque in the soft light of declining day, and all around was so still that we could hear the voices of bowlers who were lingering upon the green, off at the north side of the house, and retired from the highway by an intervening garden. The varied tones of animation, and the phrases uttered by the players, on different parts of the green, came through the quiet air with a cheery ring. The language of the bowling-green sounds very quaint to people unused to the game. "Too much land, James!" cries one. "Bravo, bully-bowl! That's th' first wood! Come again for more!" cries another. "Th' wrong bias, John!" "How's that?" "A good road; but it wants legs! Narrow; narrow, o' to pieces!" These, and such like phrases of the game, came distinctly from the green into the highway that quiet evening. And here I am reminded, as I write, that the philosophic Doctor Dalton was a regular bowler upon Tattersall's green, at Old Trafford. These things, however, are all aside from the little matters which I wish to tell.

As we stood by the watering-trough, listening to the voices of the bowlers, and to the occasional ringing of bells mingled with a low buzz of merriment inside the house, there were many travellers went by. They came, nearly all of them, from the Manchester side; sometimes three or four in company, and sometimes a lonely straggler. Some of them had poor-looking little bundles in their hands; and, with a few exceptions, their dress, their weary gait, and dispirited looks led me to think that many of them were unemployed factory operatives, who had been wandering away to beg where they would not be known. I have met so many shame-faced, melancholy people in that condition during the last few months, that, perhaps, I may have somewhat over judged the number of these that belongs to that class. But, in two or three cases, little snatches of conversation, uttered by them as they went by, plainly told that, so far as the speakers went, it was so; and, at last, a little thing befell, which, I am sure, represented the condition of many a thousand more in Lancashire just now. Three young women stopped on the footpath in front of the inn, close to the place where we stood, and began to talk together in a very free, open way, quite careless of being overheard. One of them was a stout, handsome young woman, about twenty-three. Her dress was of light printed stuff, clean and good. Her round, ruddy arms, her clear blond complexion, and the bright expression of her full open countenance, all indicated health and good-nature. I guessed from her conversation, as well as from her general appearance, that she was a factory operative in full employ--though that is such a rare thing in these parts now. The other two looked very poor and downhearted. One was a short, thick-set girl, seemingly not twenty years of age; her face was sad, and she had very little to say. The other was a thin, dark-haired, cadaverous woman, above thirty years of age, as I supposed; her shrunk visage was the picture of want, and her frank, child-like talk showed great simplicity of character. The weather had been wet for some days previous; and the clothing of the two looked thin, and shower-stained. It had evidently been worn a good while; and the colours were faded. Each of them wore a shivery bit of shawl, in which their hands were folded, as if to keep them warm. The handsome lass, who seemed to be in good employ, knew them both; but she showed an especial kindness towards the eldest of them.

As these two stood talking to their friend, we did not take much notice of what they were saying until two other young women came slowly from townwards, looking poor, and tired, and ill, like the first. These last comers instantly recognised two of those who stood talking together in front of the inn, and one of them said to the other, "Eh, sitho; there's Sarah an' Martha here! . . . Eh, lasses; han yo bin a-beggin' too?" "Ay, lass; we han;" replied the thin, dark complexioned woman; "Ay, lass; we han. Aw've just bin tellin' Ann, here. Aw never did sich a thing i' my life afore--never! But it's th' first time and th' last for me,--it is that! Aw'll go whoam; an' aw'll dee theer, afore aw'll go a-beggin' ony moor, aw will for sure! Mon, it's sich a nasty, dirty job; aw'd as soon clem! . . . See yo, lasses; we set off this mornin'--Martha an' me, we set eawt this mornin' to go to Gorton Tank, becose we yerd that it wur sich a good place. But one doesn't know wheer to go these times; an' one doesn't like to go a-beggin' among folk at they known. Well, when we coom to Gorton we geet twopence-hawpenny theer; an' that wur o'. Neaw, there's plenty moor beggin' besides us. Well, at after that twopence-hawpenny, we geet twopence moor, an' that's o' at we'n getten. But, eh, lasses, when aw coom to do it, aw hadn't th' heart to as for nought; aw hadn't for sure. . . . Martha an' me's walked aboon ten mile iv we'n walked a yard; an' we geet weet through th' first thing; an' aw wur ill when we set off, an' so wur Martha, too; aw know hoo wur, though hoo says nought. Well; we coom back through t' teawn; an' we were both on us fair stagged up. Aw never were so done o'er i' my life, wi' one thing an' another. So we co'de a-seein' Ann here; an' hoo made us a rare good baggin'--th' lass did. See yo; aw wur fit to drop o'th flags afore aw geet that saup o' warm tay into mo--aw wur for sure! An' neaw, hoo's come'd a gate wi' us hitherto, an' hoo would have us to have a glass o' warm ale a- piece at yon heawse lower deawn a bit; an' aw dar say it'll do mo good, aw getten sich a cowd; but, eh dear, it's made mo as mazy as a tup; an' neaw, hoo wants us to have another afore we starten off whoam. But it's no use; we mun' be gooin' on. Aw'm noan used to it, an' aw connot ston it. Aw'm as wake as a kittlin' this minute."

Ann, who had befriended them in this manner, was the handsome young woman who seemed to be in work; and now, the poor woman who had been telling the story, laid her hand upon her friend's shoulder and said, "Ann, thae's behaved very weel to us o' roads; an' neaw, lass, go thi ways whoam, an' dunnut fret abeawt us, mon. Aw feel better neaw, aw do for sure. We's be reet enough to-morn, lass. Mon, there's awlus some way shap't. That tay's done me a deeol o' good. . . . Go thi ways whoam, Ann; neaw do; or else aw shan't be yezzy abeawt tho!" But Ann, who was wiping her eyes with her apron, replied, "Naw, naw; aw will not go yet, Sarah!" . . . And then she began to cry, "Eh, lasses; aw dunnot like to see yo o' this shap--aw dunnot for sure! Besides, yo'n bin far enough today. Come back wi' me. Aw connot find reawm for both on yo; but thee come back wi' me, Sarah. Aw'll find thee a good bed:

an' thae'rt welcome to a share o' what there is--as welcome as th' fleawers i May--thae knows that. Thae'rt th' owdest o' th' two; an thae'rt noan fit to trawnce up an' deawn o' this shap. Come back to eawr heawse; an' Martha'll go forrud to Stopput, (Stockport,)--winnot tho, Martha! . . . Thae knows, Martha," continued she, "thae knows, Martha, thae munnot think nought at me axin' Sarah, an' noan o' thee. Yo should both on yo go back iv aw'd reawm,--but aw haven't. Beside, thae'rt younger an' strunger than hoo is." " Eh, God bless tho, lass," replied Martha, "aw know o' abeawt it. Aw'd rayther Sarah would stop, for hoo'll be ill. Aw can go forrud by mysel', weel enough. It's noan so fur, neaw." But, here, Sarah, the eldest of the three, laid her hand once more upon the shoulder of her friend, and said in an earnest tone, "Ann! it will not do, my lass! Go aw MUN! I never wur away fro whoam o' neet i my life,--never! Aw connot do it, mon! Beside, thae knows, aw've laft yon lad, an' never a wick soul wi' him! He'd fret hissel' to deoth this neet, mon, if aw didn't go whoam! Aw couldn't sleep a wink for thinkin' abeawt him! Th' child would be fit to start eawt o'th heawse i'th deead time o'th neet a-seechin' mo,--aw know he would! . . . Aw mun go, mon:

God bless tho, Ann; aw'm obleeged to thee o' th' same. But, thae knows heaw it is. Aw mun goo!"

Here the omnibus came up, and I rode back to Manchester. The whole conversation took up very little more time than it will take to read it; but I thought it worth recording, as characteristic of the people now suffering in Lancashire from no fault of their own. I know the people well. The greatest number of them would starve themselves to that degree that they would not be of much more physical use in this world, before they would condescend to beg. But starving to death is hard work. What will winter bring to them when severe weather begins to tell upon constitutions lowered in tone by a starvation diet--a diet so different to what they have been used to when in work? What will the 1s. 6d. a-head weekly do for them in that hard time? If something more than this is not done for them, when more food, clothing, and fire are necessary to everybody, calamities may arise which will cost England a hundred times more than a sufficient relief--a relief worthy of those who are suffering, and of the nation they belong to--would have cost. In the meantime the cold wings of winter already begin to overshadow the land; and every day lost involves the lives, or the future usefulness, of thousands of our best population.

CHAPTER XXIII.

WANDERING MINSTRELS; OR, WAILS OF THE WORKLESS POOR.

"For whom the heart of man shuts out, Straightway the heart of God takes in, And fences them all round about With silence, 'mid the world's loud din. And one of his great charities Is music; and it doth not scorn To close the lids upon the eyes Of the weary and forlorn." --JAMES RUSSEL LOWELL.

There is one feature of the distress in Lancashire which was seen strikingly upon the streets of our large towns during some months of 1862. I allude to the wandering minstrelsy of the unemployed. Swarms of strange, shy, sad-looking singers and instrumental performers, in the work-worn clothing of factory operatives, went about the busy city, pleading for help in touching wails of simple song--like so many wild birds driven by hard weather to the haunts of man. There is something instructive, as well as affecting, in this feature of the troubled time. These wanderers are only a kind of representative overflow of a vast number whom our streets will never see. Any one well acquainted with Lancashire, will know how widespread the study of music is among its working population. Even the inhabitants of our large towns know something more about this now than they knew a few months ago. I believe there is no part of England in which the practice of sacred music is so widely and lovingly pursued amongst the working people as in the counties of Lancashire and Yorkshire. There is no part of England where, until lately, there have been so many poor men's pianos, which have been purchased by a long course of careful savings from the workman's wages. These, of course, have mostly been sold during the hard times to keep life in the owner and his family. The great works of

Handel, Haydn, Beethoven, and Mozart have solaced the toil of thousands of the poorest working people of Lancashire. Anybody accustomed to wander among the moorlands of the country will remember how common it is to hear the people practising sacred music in their lonely cottages. It is not uncommon to meet working men wandering over the wild hills, "where whip and heather grow," with their musical instruments, to take part in some village oratorio many miles away. "That reminds me," as tale-tellers say, of an incident among the hills, which was interesting, though far from singular in my experience.

Up in the forest of Rosendale, between Derply Moor and the wild bill called Swinshaw, there is a little lone valley, a green cup in the mountains, called "Dean." The inhabitants of this valley are so notable for their love of music, that they are known all through the vales of Rosendale as "Th' Deighn Layrocks," or "The Larks of Dean." In the twilight of a glorious Sunday evening, in the height of summer, I was roaming over the heathery waste of Swinshaw, towards Dean, in company with a musical friend of mine, who lived in the neighbouring clough, when we saw a little crowd of people coming down a moorland slope, far away in front of us. As they drew nearer, we found that many of them had musical instruments, and when we met, my friend recognised them as working people living in the district, and mostly well known to him. He inquired where they had been; and they told him that they had "bin to a bit ov a sing deawn i'th Deighn." "Well," said he, "can't we have a tune here?" "Sure, yo con, wi' o' th' plezzur i'th world," replied he who acted as spokesman; and a low buzz of delighted consent ran through the rest of the company. They then ranged themselves in a circle around their conductor, and they played and sang several fine pieces of psalmody upon the heather-scented mountain top. As those solemn strains floated over the wild landscape, startling the moorfowl untimely in his nest, I could not help thinking of the hunted Covenanters of Scotland. The all-together of that scene upon the mountains, "between the gloaming and the mirk," made an impression upon me which I shall not easily forget. Long after we parted from them we could hear their voices, softening in sound as the distance grew, chanting on their way down the echoing glen, and the effect was wonderfully fine. This little incident upon the top of Swinshaw is representative of things which often occur in the country parts of Lancashire, showing how widespread the love of music is among the working classes there. Even in great manufacturing towns, it is very common, when passing cotton mills at work, to hear some fine psalm tune streaming in chorus from female voices, and mingling with the spoom of thousands of spindles. The "Larks of Dean," like the rest of Lancashire operatives, must have suffered in this melancholy time; but I hope that the humble musicians of our county will never have occasion to hang their harps upon the willows.

Now, when fortune has laid such a load of sorrow upon the working people of Lancashire, it is a sad thing to see so many workless minstrels of humble life "chanting their artless notes in simple guise" upon the streets of great towns, amongst a kind of life they are little used to. There is something very touching, too, in their manner and appearance. They may be ill-shod and footsore; they may be hungry, and sick at heart, and forlorn in countenance, but they are almost always clean and wholesome-looking in person. They come singing in twos and threes, and sometimes in more numerous bands, as if to keep one another in countenance. Sometimes they come in a large family all together, the females with their hymn-books, and the men with their different musical instruments,--bits of pet salvage from the wrecks of cottage homes. The women have sometimes children in their arms, or led by the hand;

and they sometimes carry music-books for the men. I have seen them, too, with little handkerchiefs of rude provender for the day. As I said before, they are almost invariably clean in person, and their clothing is almost always sound and seemly in appearance, however poor and scanty. Amongst these poor wanderers there is none of the reckless personal negligence and filth of hopeless reprobacy; neither is there a shadow of the professional ostentation of poverty amongst them. Their faces are sad, and their manners very often singularly shame- faced and awkward; and any careful observer would see at a glance that these people were altogether unused to the craft of the trained minstrel of the streets. Their clear, healthy complexion, though often touched with pallor, their simple, unimportunate demeanour, and the general rusticity of their appearance, shows them to be

"Suppliants who would blush To wear a tatter'd garb, however coarse; Whom famine cannot reconcile to filth; Who ask with painful shyness, and refused, Because deserving, silently retire."

The females, especially the younger ones, generally walk behind, blushing and hiding themselves as much as possible. I have seen the men sometimes walk backwards, with their faces towards those who were advancing, as if ashamed of what they were doing. And thus they went wailing through the busy streets, whilst the listening crowd looks on them pityingly and wonderingly, as if they were so many hungry shepherds from the mountains of Calabria. This flood of strange minstrels partly drowned the slang melodies and the monotonous strains of ordinary street musicians for a while. The professional gleeman "paled his ineffectual fire" before these mournful songsters. I think there never was so much sacred music heard upon the streets of Manchester before. With the exception of a favourite glee now and then, their music consisted chiefly of fine psalm tunes--often plaintive old strains, known and welcome to all, because they awaken tender and elevating remembrances of life. "Burton," "French," "Kilmarnock," "Luther's Hymn," the grand "Old Hundred," and many other fine tunes of similar character, have floated daily in the air of our city, for months together. I am sure that this choice does not arise from the minstrels themselves having craft enough to select "a mournful muse, soft pity to infuse." It is the kind of music which has been the practice and pleasure of their lives, and it is a fortuitous thing that now, in addition to its natural plaintiveness, the sad necessity of the times lends a tender accompaniment to their simplest melody. I doubt very much whether Leech's minor tunes were ever heard upon our streets till lately. Leech was a working man, born near the hills, in Lancashire; and his anthems and psalm tunes are great favourites among the musical population, especially in the country districts. Leech's harp was tuned by the genius of sorrow. Several times lately I have heard the tender complaining notes of his psalmody upon the streets of the city. About three months ago I heard one of his most pathetic tunes sung in the market-place by an old man and two young women. The old man's dress had the peculiar hue and fray of factory work upon it, and he had a pair of clogs upon his stockingless feet. They were singing one of Leech's finest minor tunes to Wesley's hymn:-

"And am I born to die, To lay this body down? And must my trembling spirit fly Into a world unknown? A land of deepest shade, Unpierced by human thought; The dreary country of the dead Where all things are forgot."

It is a tune often sung by country people in Lancashire at funerals; and, if I remember right, the same melody is cut upon Leech's gravestone in the old Wesleyan Chapel-yard, at Rochdale. I saw a company of minstrels of the same class going through Brown Street, the other day, playing and singing,

"In darkest shades, if Thou appear, My dawning is begun."

The company consisted of an old man, two young men, and three young women. Two of the women had children in their arms. After I had listened to them a little while, thinking the time and the words a little appropriate to their condition, I beckoned to one of the young men, who came "sidling" slowly up to me. I asked him where they came from, and he said, "Ash'n." In answer to another question, he said, "We're o' one family. Me an' yon tother's wed. That's his wife wi' th' chylt in her arms, an' hur wi' th' plod shawl on's mine." I asked if the old man was his father. "Ay," replied he, "we're o' here, nobbut two. My mother's ill i' bed, an' one o' my sisters is lookin' after her." " Well, an' heaw han yo getten on?" said I. "Oh, we'n done weel; but we's come no moor," replied he. Another day, there was an instrumental band of these operatives playing sacred music close to the Exchange lamp. Amongst the crowd around, I met with a friend of mine. He told me that the players were from Staleybridge. They played some fine old tunes, by desire, and, among the rest, they played one called "Warrington. "When they had played it several times over, my friend turned to me and said, "That tune was composed by a Rev. Mr Harrison, who was once minister of Cross Street Unitarian Chapel, in Manchester; and, one day, an old weaver, who had come down from the hills, many miles, staff in hand, knocked at the minister's door, and asked if there was 'a gentleman co'de' Harrison lived theer?' 'Yes.' 'Could aw see him?' 'Yes.' When the minister came to the door, the old weaver looked hard at him, for a minute, and said, 'Are yo th' mon 'at composed that tune co'de Worrington?' 'Yes,' replied the minister, 'I believe I am.' 'Well,' said the old weaver, 'give me your hond! It's a good un!' He then shook hands with him heartily again, and saying, 'Well, good day to yo,' he went his way home again, before the old minister could fairly collect his scattered thoughts."

I do not know how it is that these workless minstrels are gradually becoming rarer upon the streets than they were a few months ago. Perhaps it is because the unemployed are more liberally relieved now than they were at first. I know that now many who have concealed their starving condition are ferreted out and relieved as far as possible. Many of these street wanderers have gone home again disgusted, to pinch out the hard time in proud obscurity; and there are some, no doubt, who have wandered away to other parts of England. Of these last, we may naturally expect that a few may become so reconciled to a life of wandering minstrelsy that they may probably never return to settled labour again. But "there's a divinity that shapes our ends, rough-hew them how we will." Let us trust that the Great Creator may comfort and relieve them, "according to their several necessities, giving them patience under their sufferings, and a happy issue out of all their afflictions."

LETTER AND SPEECHES UPON THE COTTON FAMINE
LETTERS OF A LANCASHIRE LAD ON THE COTTON FAMINE.

The following extracts are from the letters of Mr. John Whittaker, "A Lancashire Lad," one of the first writers whose appeals through the press drew serious attention to the great distress in Lancashire during the Cotton Famine. There is no doubt that his letters in The Times, and to the Lord Mayor of London, led to the Mansion House Fund. In The Times of April 14, 1862, appeared the first of a series of letters, pleading the cause of the distressed operatives. He said:-

"I am living in the centre of a vast district where there are many cotton mills, which in ordinary times afford employment to many thousands of 'hands,' and food to many more thousands of mouths. With rare exceptions, quietness reigns at all those mills. . . . It may be that our material atmosphere is somewhat brighter than it was, but our social atmosphere is much darker and denser. Hard times have come; and we have had them sufficiently long to know what they mean. We have fathers sitting in the house at mid-day, silent and glum, while children look wistfully about, and sometimes whimper for bread which they cannot have. We have the same fathers who, before hard times came, were proud men, who would have thought 'beggar' the most opprobrious epithet you could have hit them with; but who now are made humble by the sight of wife and children almost starving, and who go before 'relief committees,' and submit to be questioned about their wants with a patience and humility which it is painful, almost schocking, to witness, And some others of these fathers turn out in the morning with long besoms as street-sweepers, while others again go to breaking stones in the town's yard or open road-side, where they are unprotected from the keen east winds, which add a little more to the burden of misery which they have to bear just now. But, harder even than this, our factory-women and girls have had to turn out; and, plodding a weary way from door to door, beg a bit of bread or a stray copper, that they may eke out the scanty supply at home. Only the other day, while taking a long stroll in the country lying about the town in which I live, I met a few of these factory-girls, and was stopped by their not very beggar-like question of 'Con yo help us a bit?' They were just such as my own sisters; and as I saw and heard them, I was almost choked as I fancied my sisters come to such a pass as that. 'Con yo help us a bit?' asked these factory girls.

. . . I have heard of ladies whose whole lives seem to be but a changing from one kind of pleasure to another; who suffer chiefly from what they call ennui, (a kind of disease from which my sisters are not likely to suffer at all,) and to whom a new pleasure to enjoy would be something like what a new world to conquer would be to Alexander. Why should they not hear our Lancashire girls' cry of 'Con yo help us a bit?' Why should not they be reminded that these girls in cotton gowns and wooden clogs are wending their way towards the same heaven--or, alas, towards the same hell--whither wend all the daughters of Eve, no matter what their outer condition and dress? Why should not they be asked to think how these striving girls have to pray daily, 'Lead us not into temptation,' while temptations innumerable stand everywhere about them?

Those of us who are men would rather do much than let our sisters go begging. May not some of us take to doing more to prevent it? I remember some poetry about the

'Sister bloodhounds, Want and Sin,'

and know that they hunt oftener together than singly. We have felt the fangs of the first:

upon how many of us will the second pounce?"

In a second letter, inserted in The Times of April 22, 1862, the same writer says:--"Even during the short time which has elapsed since I wrote last week, many things have combined to show that the distress is rapidly increasing, and that there is a pressing need that we should go beyond the borders of our own county for help. . . . I remember what I have read of the Godlike in man, and I look with a strange feeling upon the half-famished creatures I see hourly about me. I cannot pass through a street but I see evidences of deep distress. I cannot sit at home half-an-hour without having one or more coming to ask for bread to eat. But what comes casually before me is as nothing when compared with that deeper distress which can only be seen by those who seek it. . . . There have been families who have been so reduced that the only food they have had has been a porridge made of Indian meal. They could not afford oatmeal, and even of their Indian meal porridge they could only afford to have two meals a day. They have been so ashamed of their coarser food that they have done all that was possible to hide their desperate state from those about them. It has only been by accident that it has been found out, and then they have been caught hurriedly putting away the dishes that contained their loathsome food. A woman, whose name I could give, and whose dwelling I could point to, was said not only to be in deep distress, but to be also ill of fever. She was visited. On entering the lower room of the house, the visitors saw that there was not a scrap of furniture; the woman, fever-stricken, sat on an orange-box before a low fire; and to prevent the fire from going quite out, she was pulling her seat to pieces for fuel bit by bit. The visitors looked upstairs. There was no furniture there-- only a bit of straw in a corner, which served as the bed of the woman's four children. In another case a woman, who was said to be too weak to apply for relief, was visited. Her husband had been out of work a long time by reason of his illness; he was now of a fashion recovered, and had gone off to seek for work. He left his wife and three children in their cellar-home. The wife was very near her confinement, and had not tasted food for two or three days. . . . There are in this town some hundreds of young single women who have been self-dependent, but who are now entirely without means. Nearly all of these are good English girls, who have quietly fought their own life-battle, but who now have hard work to withstand the attacks this grim poverty is making. I am told of a case in which one of these girls was forced to become one of that class of whom poor Hood sang in his 'Bridge of Sighs.' She was an orphan, had no relations here, and was tossed about from place to place till she found her way to a brothel. Thank God, she has been rescued. Our relief fund has been the means of relieving her from that degradation; but cannot those who read my letter see how strong are the temptations which their want places in the way of these poor girls!"

On 25th April a number of city merchants, most of whom were interested in the cotton manufacture, waited upon the Lord Mayor of London, with a view to interest him, and through him the public at large, in the increasing distress among the operative population in the manufacturing districts of Lancashire. Previous to this, the "Lancashire Lad" had made a private appeal, by letter, to the Lord Mayor, in which he said:-

"Local means are nearly exhausted, and I am convinced that if we have not help from without, our condition will soon be more desperate than I or any one else who possesses human feelings can wish it to become. To see the homes of those whom we know and respect, though they are but working men, stripped of every bit of furniture--to see long-cherished books and pictures sent one by one to the pawn-shop, that food may be had--and to see that food almost loathsome in kind, and insufficient in quantity,--are hard, very hard things to bear. But those are not the worst things. In many of our cottage homes there is now nothing left by the pawning of which a few pence may be raised, and the mothers and sisters of we 'Lancashire lads' have turned out to beg, and ofttimes knock at the doors of houses in which there is as much destitution as there is in our own; while the fathers and the lads themselves think they are very fortunate if they can earn a shilling or two by street-sweeping or stone breaking. . . . Will you not do for us what you have done for others--become the recipient of whatever moneys those who are inclined to help us may send to you?"

The Lord Mayor, having listened to the deputation, read them the personal appeal, and, "before separating, the deputation engaged to form themselves into a provisional committee, to correspond with any local one which circumstances might render it desirable to set on foot in some central part of the distressed districts." Immediately afterwards, the Lord Mayor, on taking his seat in the justice-room, stated that "he was ready, with the assistance of the gentlemen of the deputation, to act in the way desired. . . . He could not himself take any part in the distribution. All he could do was to be the medium of transmission; and as soon as he knew that some organisation had been formed, either in the great city of Manchester, or in some other part of Lancashire, in which the public might feel confidence, he should be ready to send the small sums he had already received, and any others that might be intrusted to him from time to time." And thus originated the first general subscription for the cotton operatives, and which, before it closed, reached the magnificent sum of 528 pounds,336, 9s. 9d.

MR COBDEN'S SPEECH ON THE COTTON FAMINE.

On the 29th of April 1862, a meeting of gentlemen residents, called by Thomas Goadsby, Esq., Mayor of Manchester, was held in the Town Hall of that city, to consider the propriety of forming a relief committee. "'The late Mr Richard Cobden, M.P., attended, and recommended a bold appeal to the whole country, declaring with prophetic keenness of vision that not less than 1,000,000 pounds would be required to carry the suffering operatives through the crisis, whilst the subscriptions up to that date amounted only to 180,000 pounds." On the motion of a vote of thanks to the Mayor of Manchester, who was retiring from the mayoralty, Mr Cobden said:-

"Before that resolution is passed, I will take the opportunity of making an observation. I have had the honour of having my name added to this committee, and the first thing I asked of my neighbour here was--'What are the functions of the general committee?' And I have heard that they amount to nothing more than to attend here once a month, and receive the report of the executive committee as to the business done and the distribution of the funds. I was going to suggest to you whether the duties of the general committee might not be very much enlarged-- whether it might not be employed very usefully in increasing the amount of subscriptions. I think all our experience must have taught us that, with the very best cause in the world in hand, the success of a public subscription depends very much upon the amount of activity in those who solicit it; and I think, in order to induce us to make a general and national effort to raise additional funds in this great emergency, it is only necessary to refer to and repeat one or two facts that have been stated in this report just read to us. I find it stated that it is estimated that the loss of wages at present is at the rate of 136,094 pounds per week, and there is no doubt that the savings of the working classes are almost exhausted. Now, 136,094 pounds per week represents upwards of 7,000,000 pounds sterling per annum, and that is the rate at which the deduction is now being made from the wages of labour in this district.

I see it stated in this report that the resources which this committee can at present foresee that it will possess to relieve this amount of distress are 25,000 pounds a month for the next five months, which is at the rate of 300,000 pounds per annum; so that we foresee at present the means of affording a relief of something less than five per cent upon the actual amount of the loss of wages at present incurred by the working classes of this country. But I need not tell honourable gentlemen present, who are so practically acquainted with this district, that that loss of seven millions in wages per annum is a very imperfect measure of the amount of suffering and loss which will be inflicted on this community three or four months hence. It may be taken to be 10,000,000 pounds; and that 10,000,000 pounds of loss of wages before the next spring is by no means a measure of the loss this district will incur; for you must take it that the capitalists will be incurring also a loss on their fixed machinery and buildings; and though perhaps not so much as that of the labourer, it will be a very large amount, and possibly, in the opinion of some people, will very nearly approach it.

That is not all:

Mr Farnall has told us that at present the increase of the rates in this district is at the rate of 10,000 pounds per week. That will be at the rate of half a million per annum, and, of course, if this distress goes on, that rate must be largely increased, perhaps doubled. This shows the amount of pressure which is threatening this immediate district. I have always been of opinion that this distress and suffering must be cumulative to a degree which few people have ever foreseen, because your means of meeting the difficulty will diminish just in proportion as the difficulty will increase. Mr Farnall has told us that one-third of the rateable property will fall out of existence, as it were, and future rates must be levied upon two-thirds. But that will be by no means the measure of the condition of things two or three months hence, because every additional rate forces out of existence a large amount of saleable property; and the more you increase your rates the more you diminish the area over which those rates are to be productive. This view of the case has a very important bearing, also, upon the condition of the shop-keeping class as well as the classes of mill-owners and manufacturers who have not a large amount of floating capital. There is no doubt but a very large amount of the shopkeeping class are rapidly falling into the condition of the unemployed labourers.

When I was at Rochdale the other day, I heard a very sorrowful example of it. There was a poor woman who kept a shop, and she was threatened with a distraint for her poor-rate. She sold the Sunday clothes of her son to pay the poor-rate, and she received a relief- ticket when she went to leave her rate. That is a sad and sorrowful example, but I am afraid it will not be a solitary one for a long time. Then you have the shopkeeping class descending to the rank of the operatives. It must be so. Withdraw the custom of 7,000,000 pounds per annum, which has ceased to be paid in wages, from the shopkeepers, and the consequence must present itself to any rational mind. We have then another class--the young men of superior education employed in warehouses and counting-houses. A great number of these will rapidly sink to the condition in which you find the operative classes. All this will add to the distress and the embarrassment of this part of the kingdom. Now, to meet this state of things you have the poor-law relief, which is the only relief we can rely upon, except that which comes from our own voluntary exertions. Well, but any one who has read over this report of Mr Farnall, just laid before us, must see how inadequate this relief must be. It runs up from one shilling and a half-penny in the pound to one shilling and fourpence or one shilling and fivepence; there is hardly one case in which the allowance is as much as two shillings per week for each individual--I won't call them paupers-- each distressed individual.

Now, there is one point to which I would wish to bring the attention of the committee in reference to this subject--it is a most important one, in my appreciation. In ordinary times, when you give relief to the poor, that relief being given when the great mass of workpeople are in full employment, the measure of your relief to an isolated family or two that may be in distress is by no means the measure of the amount of their subsistence, because we all know that in prosperous times, when the bulk of the working people are employed, they are always kind to each other. The poor, in fact, do more to relieve the poor than any other class. A working man and his family out of employment in prosperous times could get a meal at a neighbour's house, just as we, in our class, could get a meal at a neighbour's house if it was a convenience to us in making a journey. But recollect, now the whole mass of the labouring and working population is brought down to one sad level of destitution, and what you allow them from the poor-rates, and what you allow them from these voluntary subscriptions, are actually the measure of all that they will obtain for their subsistence. And that being so general, producing a great depression of spirits, as well as physical prostration, you are in great danger of the health and strength of this community suffering, unless something more be done to meet the case than I fear is yet provided for it. All this brings me to this conclusion--that something more must be done by this general committee than has been done, to awaken the attention of the public generally to the condition of this part of the country. It is totally exceptional. The state of things has no parallel in all history. It is impossible you could point out to me another case, in which, in a limited sphere, such as we have in Lancashire, and in the course of a few months, there has been a cessation of employment at the rate of 7,000,000 pounds sterling per annum in wages. There has been nothing like it in the history of the world for its suddenness, for the impossibility of dealing with it, or managing it in the way of an effective remedy.

Well, the country at large must be made acquainted with these facts. How is that to be done? It can only be by the diffusion of information from this central committee. An appeal must be made to the whole country, if this great destitution is to be met in any part by voluntary aid. The nation at large must be made fully acquainted with the exigency of the case, and we must be reminded that a national responsibility rests upon us. I will, therefore, suggest that this general committee should be made a national committee, and we shall then get rid of this little difficulty with the Lord Mayor. We shall want all the co-operation of the Lord Mayor and the city of London; and I say that this committee, instead of being a Manchester or Lancashire central committee, should be made a national committee; that from this should go forth invitations to all parts of the country, beginning with the lords-lieutenant, inviting them to be vice-presidents of this committee. Let the noble Lord continue to be at the head of the general committee--the national committee--and invite every mayor to take part. We are going to have new mayors in the course of the week, and, though I am sorry to lose our present one, yet when new mayors come in, they may be probably more ready to take up a new undertaking than if they had just been exhausted with a years labour. Let every mayor in the kingdom be invited to become a member of this committee. Let subscription-circulars be despatched to them asking them to organise a committee in every borough; and let there be a secretary and honorary secretary employed. Through these bodies you might communicate information, and counteract those misrepresentations that have been made with regard to the condition of this district.

You might, if necessary, send an ambassador to some of those more important places; but better still, if you could induce them to send some one here to look into the state of things for themselves; because I am sure if they did, so far from finding the calumnies that have been uttered against the propertied classes in this county being well founded, they would find instances--and not a few--of great liberality and generosity, such as I think would surprise any one who visited this district from the southern part of the kingdom.

This would only be done by an active effort from the centre here, and I submit that we shall not be doing justice to this effort unless we give to the whole country an opportunity of co-operating in that way, and throw upon every part of the kingdom a share of the responsibility of this great crisis and emergency. I submit that there is every motive why this community, as well as the whole kingdom, should wish to preserve this industrious population in health and in the possession of their energies. There is every motive why we should endeavour to keep this working population here rather than drive them away from here, as you will do if they are not sufficiently fed and clothed during the next winter. They will be wanted again if this district is to revive, as we all hope and believe it will revive. Your fixed capital here is of no use without the population. It is of no use without your raw material. Lancashire is the richest county in the kingdom when its machinery is employed; it is the poorest county in the kingdom when its machinery and fixed capital are paralysed, as at present. Therefore, I say it is the interest, not only of this community, but of the kingdom, that this population should be preserved for the time--I hope not a distant time--when the raw material of their industry will be supplied to this region.

I submit; then, to the whole kingdom--this district as well as the rest--that it will be advisable, until Parliament meets, that such an effort should be made as will make a national subscription amount probably to 1,000,000 pounds. Short of that, it would be utterly insufficient for the case; and I believe that, with an energetic appeal made to the whole country, and an effort organised such as I have indicated, such an amount might be raised."

SPEECH OF THE EARL OF DERBY
AT THE COUNTY MEETING, ON THE 2D DECEMBER 1863. THE EARL OF SEFTON IN THE CHAIR.

The thirteen hundred circulars issued by the Earl of Sefton, Lord- Lieutenant of Lancashire, "brought together such a gathering of rank, and wealth, and influence, as is not often to be witnessed; and the eloquent advocate of class distinctions and aristocratic privileges (the Earl of Derby) became on that day the powerful and successful representative of the poor and helpless." Called upon by the chairman, the Earl of Derby said:-

"My Lord Sefton, my Lords and Gentlemen,--We are met together upon an occasion which must call forth the most painful, and at the same time ought to excite, and I am sure will excite, the most kindly feelings of our human nature. We are met to consider the best means of palliating--would to God that I could say removing!--a great national calamity, the like whereof in modern times has never been witnessed in this favoured land--a calamity which it was impossible for those who are the chief sufferers by it to foresee, or, if they had foreseen, to have taken any steps to avoid--a calamity which, though shared by the nation at large, falls more peculiarly and with the heaviest weight upon this hitherto prosperous and wealthy district--a calamity which has converted this teeming hive of industry into a stagnant desert of compulsory inaction and idleness--a calamity which has converted that which was the source of our greatest wealth into the deepest abyss of impoverishment--a calamity which has impoverished the wealthy, which has reduced men of easy fortunes to the greatest straits, which has brought distress upon those who have hitherto been somewhat above the world by the exercise of frugal industry, and which has reduced honest and struggling poverty to a state of absolute and humiliating destitution. Gentlemen, it is to meet this calamity that we are met together this day, to add our means and our assistance to those efforts which have been so nobly made throughout the country generally, and, I am bound to say, in this county also, as I shall prove to you before I conclude my remarks. Gentlemen, I know how impossible it is by any figures to convey an idea of the extent of the destitution which now prevails, and I know also how impatient large assemblies are of any extensive use of figures, or even of figures at all; but at the same time, it is impossible for me to lay before you the whole state of the case, in opening this resolution, and asking you to resolve with regard to the extent of the distress which now prevails, without trespassing on your attention by a few, and they shall be a very few, figures, which shall show the extent, if not the pressure, throughout this district, of the present distress. And, gentlemen, I think I shall best give you an idea of the amount of distress and destitution which prevails, by very shortly comparing the state of things which existed in the districts to which I refer in the month of September 1861, as compared with the month of September 1862, and with that again only about two weeks ago, which is the latest information we have--up to the 22d of last month.

I find then, gentlemen, that in a district comprising, in round numbers, two million inhabitants--for that is about the number in that district--in the fourth week of September 1861, there were forty-three thousand five hundred persons receiving parochial relief; in the fourth week of September 1862, there were one hundred and sixty-three thousand four hundred and ninety-eight persons receiving parochial relief; and in the short space which elapsed between the last week of September and the third week of November the number of one hundred and sixty-three thousand four hundred and ninety-eight had increased to two hundred and fifty-nine thousand three hundred and eighty-five persons. Now, gentlemen, let us in the same periods compare the amount which was applied from the parochial funds to the relief of pauperism. In September 1861, the amount so applied was 2259 pounds; in September 1862, it was 9674 pounds. That is by the week. What is now the amount? In November 1862 it was 17,681 pounds for the week. The proportion of those receiving parochial relief to the total population was two and three-tenths per cent in September 1861, and eight and five-tenths per cent in September 1862, and that had become thirteen and five-tenths percent in the population in November 1862. Here, therefore, is thirteen per cent of the whole population at the present moment depending for their subsistence upon parochial relief alone. Of these two hundred and fifty-nine thousand--I give only round numbers--there were thirty-six thousand eight hundred old or infirm; there were nearly ninety-eight thousand able-bodied adults receiving parochial relief, and there were under sixteen years of age nearly twenty-four thousand persons. But it would be very far from giving you an estimate of the extent of the distress if we were to confine our observations to those who are dependent upon parochial relief alone.

We have evidence from the local committees, whom we have extensively employed, and whose services have been invaluable to us, that of persons not relieved from the poor-rates there are relieved also by local committees no fewer in this district than one hundred and seventy-two thousand persons--making a total of four hundred and thirty-one thousand three hundred and ninety-five persons out of two millions, or twenty-one and seven-tenths per cent on the whole population--that is, more than one in every five persons depend for their daily existence either upon parochial relief or public charity. Gentlemen, I have said that figures will not show sufficiently the amount of distress; nor, in the same manner, will figures show, I am happy to say, the amount that has been contributed for the relief of that distress. But let us take another test; let us examine what has been the result, not upon the poor who are dependent for their daily bread upon their daily labour, and many of whom are upon the very verge of pauperism, from day to day, but let us take a test of what has been the effect upon the well-to- do artisan, upon the frugal, industrious, saving men, who have been hitherto somewhat above the world, and I have here but an imperfect test, because I am unable to obtain the whole amount of deposits withdrawn from the savings banks, the best of all possible tests, if we could carry the account up to the present day; but I have only been able to obtain it to the middle of June last, when the distress could hardly be said to have begun, and yet I find from seven savings banks alone in this county in six months--and those months in which the distress had not reached its present height, or anything like it--there was an excess of withdrawals of deposits over the ordinary average to the amount of 71,113 pounds. This was up to June last, when, as I have said, the pressure had hardly commenced, and from that time it as been found impossible to obtain from the savings banks, who are themselves naturally unwilling to disclose this state of affairs--it has been found impossible to obtain such further returns as would enable us to present to you any proper estimate of the excess of withdrawals at present; but that they have been very large must necessarily be inferred from the great increase of distress which has taken place since the large sum I have mentioned was obtained from the banks, as representing the excess of ordinary withdrawals in June last.

Now, gentlemen, figure to yourselves, I beg of you, what a state of things that sum of 71,113 pounds, as the excess of the average withdrawals from the savings banks represents; what an amount of suffering does it picture; what disappointed hopes; what a prospect of future distress does it not bring before you for the working and industrious classes? Why, gentlemen, it represents the blighted hopes for life of many a family. It represents the small sum set apart by honest, frugal, persevering industry, won by years of toil and self-denial, in the hope of its being, as it has been in many cases before, the foundation even of colossal fortunes which have been made from smaller sums. It represents the gradual decay of the hopes for his family of many an industrious artisan. The first step in that downward progress which has led to destitution and pauperism is the withdrawal of the savings of honest industry, and that is represented in the return which I have quoted to you. Then comes the sacrifice of some little cherished article of furniture--the cutting off of some little indulgence--the sacrifice of that which gave his home an appearance of additional comfort and happiness--the sacrifice gradually, one by one, of the principal articles of furniture, till at last the well-conducted, honest, frugal, saving working man finds himself on a level with the idle, the dissipated, and the improvident--obliged to pawn the very clothes of his family- -nay, the very bedding on which he lies, to obtain the simple means of subsistence from day to day, and encountering all that difficulty and all that distress with the noble independence that would do anything rather than depend upon public or even on private charity, and in his own simple but emphatic language declaring, 'Nay, but we'll CLEM first.'

And, gentlemen, this leads me to observe upon a more gratifying point of view, that is, the noble manner, a manner beyond all praise, in which this destitution has been borne by the population of this great county. It is not the case of ordinary labourers who find themselves reduced a trifle below their former means of subsistence, but it is a reduction in the pecuniary comfort, and almost necessaries, of men who have been in the habit of living, if not in luxury, at least in the extreme of comfort--a reduction to two shillings and three shillings a week from sums which had usually amounted to twenty-five shillings, or thirty shillings, or forty shillings; a cutting off of all their comforts, cutting off all their hopes of future additional comfort, or of rising in life-- aggravated by a feeling, an honourable, an honest, but at the same time a morbid feeling, of repugnance to the idea of being indebted under these circumstances to relief of any kind or description. And I may say that, among the difficulties which have been encountered by the local relief committees--no doubt there have been many of those not among the most deserving who have been clamorous for the aid held out to them--but one of the great difficulties of local relief committees has been to find out and relieve struggling and really-distressed merit, and to overcome that feeling of independence which, even under circumstances like these, leads them to shrink from being relieved by private charity. I know that instances of this kind have happened; I know that cases have occurred where it has been necessary to press upon individuals, themselves upon the point of starvation, the necessity of accepting this relief; and from this place I take the opportunity of saying, and I hope it will go far and wide, that in circumstances like the present, discreditable as habitual dependence upon parochial relief may be, it is no degradation, it is no censure, it is no possible cause of blame, that any man, however great his industry, however high his character, however noble his feeling of self-dependence, should feel himself obliged to have recourse to that Christian charity which I am sure we are all prepared to give. Gentlemen, I might perhaps here, as far as my resolution goes, close the observations I have to make to you. The resolution I have to move, indeed, is one which calls for no extensive argument; and a plain statement of facts, such as that I have laid before you, is sufficient to obtain for it your unanimous assent. The resolution is:-

"'That the manufacturing districts of Lancashire and the adjoining counties are suffering from an extent of destitution happily hitherto unknown, which has been borne by the working classes with a patient submission and resolution entitling them to the warmest sympathy of their fellow-countrymen.'

"But, gentlemen, I cannot, in the first place, lose the opportunity of asking this great assembly with what feelings this state of things should be contemplated by us who are in happier circumstances. Let me say with all reverence that it is a subject for deep national humiliation, and, above all, for deep humiliation for this great county. We have been accustomed for years to look with pride and complacency upon the enormous growth of that manufacture which has conferred wealth upon so many thousands, and which has so largely increased the manufacturing population and industry of this country. We have seen within the last twelve or fourteen years the consumption of cotton in Europe increase from fifty thousand to ninety thousand bales a week; we have seen the weight of cotton goods exported from this country in the shape of yarn and manufactured goods amount to no less than nine hundred and eighty-three million pounds in a single year. We have seen, in spite of all opposing circumstances, this trade constantly and rapidly extending; we have seen colossal fortunes made; and we have as a county, perhaps, been accustomed to look down on those less fortunate districts whose wealth and fortunes were built upon a less secure foundation; we have reckoned upon this great manufacture as the pride of our country, and as the best security against the possibility of war, in consequence of the mutual interest between us and the cotton-producing districts.

We have held that in the cotton manufacture was the pride, the strength, and the certainty of our future national prosperity and peace. I am afraid we have looked upon this trade too much in the spirit of the Assyrian monarch of old. We have said to ourselves:-- 'Is not this great Babylon, that I have built for the house of my kingdom by the might of my power, and for the honour of my majesty?' But in the hour in which the monarch used these words the word came forth, 'Thy kingdom is departed from thee!' That which was his pride became his humiliation; that which was our pride has become our humiliation and our punishment. That which was the source of our wealth--the sure foundation on which we built--has become itself the instrument of our humiliating poverty, which compels us to appeal to the charity of other counties. The reed upon which we leaned has gone through the hand that reposed on it, and has pierced us to the heart.

But, gentlemen, we have happier and more gratifying subjects of contemplation. I have pointed to the noble conduct which must make us proud of our countrymen in the mmiufacturing districts; I have pointed to the noble and heroic submission to difficulties they could never foresee, and privations they never expected to encounter; but again, we have another feeling which I am sure will not be disappointed, which the country has nobly met--that this is an opportunity providentially given to those who are blessed with wealth and fortune to show their sympathy--their practical, active, earnest sympathy--with the sufferings of their poorer brethren, and, with God's blessing, used as I trust by God's blessing it will be, it may be a link to bind together more closely than ever the various classes in this great community, to satisfy the wealthy that the poor have a claim, not only to their money, but to their sympathy-- to satisfy the poor also that the rich are not overbearing, grinding tyrants, but men like themselves, who have hearts to feel for suffering, and are prompt to use the means God has given to them for the relief of that suffering.

Gentlemen, a few words more, and I will not further trespass on your attention. But I feel myself called on, as chairman of that executive committee to which my noble friend in the chair has paid so just a compliment, to lay before you some answer to objections which have been made, and which in other counties, if not in this, may have a tendency to check the contributions which have hitherto so freely flowed in. Before doing so, allow me to say (and I can do it with more freedom, because in the, earlier stages of its organisation I was not a member of that committee) it is bare justice to them to say that there never was an occasion on which greater or more earnest efforts were made to secure that the distribution of those funds intrusted to them should be guarded against all possibility of abuse, and be distributed without the slightest reference to political or religious opinions; distributed with the most perfect impartiality, and in every locality, through the instrumentality of persons in whom the neighbourhood might repose entire confidence. Such has been our endeavour, and I think to a great extent we have been successful. I may say that, although the central executive committee is composed of men of most discordant opinions in politics and religion, nothing for a single moment has interfered with the harmony--I had almost said with the unanimity--of our proceedings. There has been nothing to produce any painful feelings among us, nor any desire on the part of the representatives of different districts to obtain an undue share for the districts they represented from the common fund.

But there are three points on which objection has being taken to the course we have adopted. One has been, that the relief we have given has not been given with a sufficiently liberal hand; the next--and I think I shall show you that these two are inconsistent, the one answering the other--is, that there has not been a sufficient pressure on the local rates; and the third is, that Lancashire has not hitherto done its duty with reference to the subscriptions from other parts of the country. Allow me a few words on each of these subjects.

First, the amount to which we have endeavoured to raise our subscriptions has been to the extent of from two shillings to two shillings and sixpence weekly per head; in this late cold weather an additional sixpence has been provided, mainly for coal and clothing. Our endeavour has been to raise the total income of each individual to at least two shillings or two shillings and sixpence a week. Now, I am told that this is a very inadequate amount, and no doubt it is an amount very far below that which many of the recipients were in the habit of obtaining. But in the first place, I think there is some misapprehension when we speak of the sum of two shillings a week. If anybody supposes that two shillings a week is the maximum to each individual, he will be greatly mistaken. Two shillings a head per week is the sum we endeavoured to arrive at as the average receipt of every man, woman, and child receiving assistance; consequently, a man and his wife with a family of three or four small children would receive, not two shillings, but ten or twelve shillings from the fund--an amount not far short of that which in prosperous times an honest and industrious labourer in other parts of the country would obtain for the maintenance of his family. I am not in the least afraid that, if we had fixed the amount at four shillings or five shillings per head, such is the liberality of the country, we should not have had sufficient means of doing so. But were we justified in doing that? If we had raised their income beyond that of the labouring man in ordinary times, we should have gone far to destroy the most valuable feeling of the manufacturing population--namely, that of honest self-reliance, and we should have done our best, to a great extent, to demoralise a large portion of the population, and induce them to prefer the wages of charitable relief to the return of honest industry. But then we are told that the rates are not sufficiently high in the distressed districts, and that we ought to raise them before we come on the fund. In the first place, we have no power to compel the guardians to raise the rates beyond that which they think sufficient for the maintenance of those to be relieved, and, naturally considering themselves the trustees of the ratepayers, they are unwilling, and, indeed, ought not to raise the amount beyond that which is called for by absolute necessity. But suppose we had raised the relief from our committee very far beyond the amount thought sufficient by the guardians, what would have been the inevitable result? Why, that the rates which it is desired to charge more heavily would have been relieved, because persons would have taken themselves off the poor-rates, and placed themselves on the charitable committee, and therefore the very object theso objectors have in view in calling for an increase of our donations would have been defeated by their own measure. I must say, however, honestly speaking all I feel, that, with regard to the amount of rates, there are some districts which have applied to us for assistance which I think have not sufficient pressure on their rates. Where I find, for example, that the total assessment on the nett rateable value does not exceed ninepence or tenpence in the pound, I really think such districts ought to be called upon to increase their rates before applying for extraneous help. But we have urged as far as we could urge--we have no power to command the guardians to be more liberal in the rate of relief, and to that extent to raise the rates in their districts.

And now a word on the subject of raising rates, because I have received many letters in which it has been said that the rates are nothing--'they are only three shillings or four shillings in the pound, while we in the agricultural districts are used to six shillings in the pound. We consider that no extraordinary rate, and it is monstrous,' they say, 'that the accumulated wealth of years in the county of Lancashire should not more largely contribute to the relief of its own distress.' I will not enter into an argument as to how far the larger amount of wages in the manufacturing districts may balance the smaller--amount of wages and the larger amount of poor-rates in the agricultural districts. I don't wish to enter into any comparison; I have seen many comparisons of this kind made, but they were full of fallacies from one end to the other. I will not waste your time by discussing them; but I ask you to consider the effect of a sudden rise of rates as a charge upon the accumulated wealth of a district. It is not the actual amount of the rates, but it is the sudden and rapid increase of the usual rate of the rates that presses most heavily on the ratepayers. In the long run, the rates must fall on real property, because all bargains between owner and occupier are made with reference to the amount of rates to be paid, and in all calculations between them, that is an element which enters into the first agreement. But when the rate is suddenly increased from one shilling to four shillings, it does not fall on the accumulated wealth or on the real property, but it falls on the occupier, the ratepayer--men, the great bulk of whom are at the present moment themselves struggling upon the verge of pauperism. Therefore, if in those districts it should appear to persons accustomed to agricultural districts that the amount of our rates was very small, I would say to them that any attempt to increase those rates would only increase the pauperism, diminish the number of solvent ratepayers, and greatly aggravate the distress. In some of the districts I think the amount of the rates quite sufficient to satisfy the most ardent advocate of high rates. For example, in the town of Ashton they have raised in the course of the year one rate of one shilling and sixpence, another of one shilling and sixpence, and a third of four shillings and sixpence, which it is hoped will carry them over the year. They have also, in addition to these rates, drawn largely on previous balances, and I am afraid have largely added to their debt. The total of what has been or will be expended, with a prospect of even a great increase, in that borough exceeds eleven shillings and elevenpence in the pound for the relief of the poor alone. And, gentlemen, this rate of four shillings and sixpence about to be levied, which ought to yield about 32,000 pounds, it is calculated will not yield 24,000 pounds. In Stockport the rate is even higher, being twelve shillings or more per pound, and there it is calculated that at the next levy the defalcations will be at least forty per cent, according to the calculation of the poor-law commissioner himself. To talk, then, of raising rates in such districts as these would be absolute insanity; and even in districts less heavily rated, any sudden attempt considerably to increase the rate would have the effect of pauperising those who are now solvent, and to augment rather than diminish the distress of the district.

The last point on which I would make an observation relates to the objection which has been taken to our proceedings, on the ground that Lancashire has not done its duty in this distress, and that consequently other parts of the country have been unduly called on to contribute to that which I don't deny properly and primarily belongs to Lancashire. Gentlemen, it is very hard to ascertain with any certainty what has been done by Lancashire, because, in the first place, the amount of local subscriptions and the amount of public contributions by themselves give no fair indication of that which really has been done by public or private charity. I don't mean to say that there are not individuals who have grossly neglected their duty in Lancashire. On the other hand, we know there are many, though I am not about to name them, who have acted with the most princely munificence, liberality, and generous feeling, involving an amount of sacrifice of which no persons out of this county can possibly have the slightest conception. I am not saying there are not instances of niggard feeling, though I am not about to name them, which really it was hardly possible to believe could exist.

Will you forgive me if I trespass for a few moments by reading two or three extracts from confidential reports made to us every week from the different districts by a gentleman whose services were placed at our disposal by the Government? These reports being, as I have said, confidential, I will not mention the names of the persons, firms, or localities alluded to, though in some instances they may be guessed at. This report was made to us on the 25th of November, and I will quote some of the remarks made in it. The writer observes:--'It must not be inferred when such remarks are absent from the reports that nothing is done. I have great difficulty sometimes in overcoming the feeling that my questions on these points are a meddlesome interference in private matters.' Bearing that remark in mind, I say here are instances which I am sure reflect as much credit on the individuals as on the interest they represent and the county to which they belong. I am sure I shall be excused for trespassing on your patience by reading a few examples. He says, under No.1,--'Nearly three thousand operatives out of the whole, most of them the hands of Messrs __ and Mr __, at his own cost, employs five hundred and fifty-five girls in sewing five days a week, paying them eightpence a day; sends seventy-six youths from thirteen to fourteen years old, and three hundred and thirty-two adults above fifteen, five days a week to school, paying them from fourpence to eightpence per day, according to age. He also pays the school pence of all the children. Mr __ has hitherto paid his people two days' wages a week, but he is now preparing to adopt a scheme like Mr __ to a great extent. I would add that, in addition to wages, Mr __ gives bread, soup, socks, and clogs. 2. Mr __ has at his own expense caused fifty to sixty dinners to be provided for sick persons every day. These consist of roast beef or mutton, soup, beef-tea, rice-puddings, wine, and porter, as ordered; and the forty visitors distribute orders as they find it necessary. Ostensibly all is done in the name of the committee; but Mr __ pays all the cost. An admirable soup kitchen is being fitted up, where the poor man may purchase a good hot meal for one penny, and either carry it away or consume it on the premises. 3. Messrs __ are giving to their hands three days' wages (about 500 pounds a week.) Messrs __ and __ are giving their one hundred and twenty hands, and Messrs their two hundred and thirty hands, two days' wages a week. I may mention that Messrs __ are providing for all their one thousand seven hundred hands. 4. A great deal of private charity exists, one firm having spent 1400 pounds in money, exclusive of weekly doles of bread. 5. Messrs __ are providing all their old hands with sufficient clothing and bedding to supply every want, so that their subscription of 50 pounds is merely nominal. 6. The ladies of the village visit and relieve privately with money, food, or clothing, or all, if needed urgently. In a few cases distraint has been threatened, but generally the poor are living rent free. 7. Payment of rent is almost unknown. The agent for several landlords assures me he could not from his receipts pay the property-tax, but no distraints are made. 8. The bulk of the rents are not collected, and distraints are unknown. 9. The millowners are chiefly cottage-owners, and are asking for no rents.'

That leads me to call your attention to the fact that, in addition to the sacrifices they are making, the millowners are themselves to a large extent the owners of cottages, and I believe, without exception, they are at the present moment receiving no rent, thereby losing a large amount of income they had a right to count upon. I know one case which is curious as showing how great is the difficulty of ascertaining what is really done. It is required in the executive committee that every committee should send in an account of the local subscriptions. We received an application from a small district where there was one mill, occupied by some young men who had just entered into the business. We returned a refusal, inasmuch as there was no local subscription; but when we came to inquire, we found that from last February, when the mill closed, these young men had maintained the whole of their hands, that they paid one-third of the rates of the whole district, and that they were at that moment suffering a yearly loss of 300 pounds in the rent of cottages for which they were not drawing a single halfpenny. That was a case in which we thought it right in the first instance to withhold any assistance, because there appeared to be no local subscription, and it shows how persons at a distance may be deceived by the want apparently of any local subscription. But I will throw out of consideration the whole of those amounts--the whole of this unparalleled munificence on the part of many manufacturers which never appears in any account whatever--I will throw out everything done in private and unostentatious charity--the supplies of bedding, clothing, food, necessaries of every description, which do not appear as public subscriptions, and will appeal to public subscriptions alone; and I will appeal to an authority which cannot, I think, be disputed--

the authority of the commissioner, Mr Farnall himself, whose services the Government kindly placed at our disposal, and of whose activity, industry, and readiness to assist us, it is difficult to speak in too high terms of praise. A better authority could not be quoted on the subject of the comparative support given in aid of this distress in Lancashire and other districts. I find that, excluding altogether the subscriptions in the Lord Mayor's Mansion House list--of which we know the general amount, but not the sources from which it is derived, or how it is expended--but excluding it from consideration, and dealing only with the funds which have been given or promised to be administered through the central executive committee, I find that, including some of the subscriptions which we know are coming in this day, the total amount which has been contributed is about 540,000 pounds. Of that amount we received--and it is a most gratifying fact--40,000 pounds from the colonies; we received from the rest of the United Kingdom 100,000 pounds; and from the county of Lancaster itself, in round numbers, 400,000 pounds out of 540,000 pounds.

Now, I hope that these figures, upon the estimate and authority of the Government poor-law commissioner, will be sufficient, at all events, to do away with the imputation that Lancashire, at this crisis, is not doing its duty. But if Lancashire has been doing its duty--if it is doing its duty--that is no reason why Lancashire should relax its efforts; and of that I trust the result of this day's proceedings will afford a sufficient testimony. We are not yet at the height of the distress. It is estimated that at the present moment there are three hundred and fifty-five thousand persons engaged in the different manufactories. Of these forty thousand only are in full work; one hundred and thirty-five thousand are at short work, and one hundred and eighty thousand are out of work altogether. In the course of the next six weeks this number is likely to be greatly increased; and the loss of wages is not less than 137,000 pounds a week. This, I say then, is a state of things that calls for the most active exertions of all classes of the community, who, I am happy to say, have responded to the call which has been made upon them most nobly, from the Queen down to the lowest individual in the community. At the commencement of the distress, the Queen, with her usual munificence, sent us a donation of 2000 pounds. The first act of His Royal Highness the Prince of Wales, upon attaining his majority, was to write from Rome, and to request that his name should be put down for 1000 pounds. And to go to the other end of the scale, I received two days ago, from Lord Shaftesbury, a donation of 1200 pounds from some thousands of working men, readers of a particular periodical which he mentioned, the British Workman. To that sum Lord Shaftesbury stated many thousands of persons had subscribed, and it embraced contributions even from the brigade of shoe-black boys.

On the part of all classes there has been the greatest liberality displayed; and I should be unjust to the working men, I should be unjust to the poor in every district, if I did not say that in proportion to their means they have contributed more than their share. In no case hardly which has come to my knowledge has there been any grudging, and in many cases I know that poor persons have contributed more than common prudence would have dictated. These observations have run to a greater extent than I had intended; but I thought it desirable that the whole case, as far as possible, should be brought before you, and I have only now earnestly to request that you will this day do your part towards the furtherance of the good work. I have no apprehension, if the distress should not last over five or six months more, that the spontaneous efforts of individuals and public bodies, and contributions received in every part of the country, will fall short of that which is needed for enabling the population to tide over this deep distress; and I earnestly hope that, if it be necessary to apply to Parliament, as a last resource, the representatives of the country will not grudge their aid; yet I do fervently hope and believe that, with the assistance of the machinery of that bill passed in Parliament last session, (the Rate in Aid Act,) which will come into operation shortly after Christmas, but could not possibly be brought into operation sooner, I do fervently hope and believe that this great manufacturing district will be spared the further humiliation of coming before Parliament, which ought to be the last resource, as a claimant, a suppliant for the bounty of the nation at large. I don't apprehend that there will be a single dissentient voice raised against the resolution which I have now the honour to move."

SONGS OF DISTRESS, CHIEFLY WRITTEN DURING THE COTTON FAMINE.

STANZAS TO MY STARVING KIN IN THE NORTH. BY ELIZA COOK.

Sad are the sounds that are breaking forth From the women and men of the brave old North! Sad are the sights for human eyes, In fireless homes, 'neath wintry skies; Where wrinkles gather on childhood's skin, And youth's "clemm'd" cheek is pallid and thin; Where the good, the honest-- unclothed, unfed, Child, mother, and father, are craving for bread! But faint not, fear not--still have trust; Your voices are heard, and your claims are just. England to England's self is true, And "God and the People" will help you through.

Brothers and sisters! full well ye have stood, While the gripe of gaunt Famine has curdled your blood! No murmur, no threat on your lips have place, Though ye look on the Hunger-fiend face to face; But haggard and worn ye silently bear, Dragging your death-chains with patience and prayer; With your hearts as loyal, your deeds as right, As when Plenty and Sleep blest your day and your night, Brothers and sisters! oh! do not believe It is Charity's GOLD ALONE ye receive. Ah, no! It is Sympathy, Feeling, and Hope, That pull out in the Life-boat to fling ye a rope.

Fondly I've lauded your wealth-winning hands, Planting Commerce and Fame throughout measureless lands; And my patriot-love, and my patriot-song, To the children of Labour will ever belong. Women and men of this brave old soil! I weep that starvation should guerdon your toil; But I glory to see ye--proudly mute-- Showing SOULS like the HERO, not FANGS like the brute. Oh! keep courage within; be the Britons ye are; HE, who driveth the storm hath His

hand on the star! England to England's sons shall be true,
And "God and the People" will carry ye through!

*

THE SMOKELESS CHIMNEY BY A LANCASHIRE LADY {1} (E.J.B.)
STRANGER!

who to buy art willing, Seek not here for talent rare; Mine's no song of love or beauty, But a tale of want and care.

Traveller on the Northern Railway! Look and learn, as on you speed; See the hundred smokeless chimneys, Learn their tale of cheerless need.

Ah! perchance the landscape fairer Charms your taste, your artist-eye; Little do you guess how dearly Costs that now unclouded sky.

"How much prettier is this county!" Says the careless passer-by; "Clouds of smoke we see no longer, What's the reason?--Tell me why.

"Better far it were, most surely, Never more such clouds to see, Bringing taint o'er nature's beauty, With their foul obscurity."

Thoughtless fair one! from yon chimney Floats the golden breath of life; Stop that current at your pleasure! Stop! and starve the child--the wife.

Ah! to them each smokeless chimney Is a signal of despair; They see hunger, sickness, ruin, Written in that pure, bright air.

"Mother! mother! see! 'twas truly Said last week the mill would stop; Mark yon chimney, nought is going, There's no smoke from 'out o'th top!'

"Father! father! what's the reason That the chimneys smokeless stand? Is it true that all through strangers, We must starve in our own land?"

Low upon her chair that mother Droops, and sighs with tearful eye; At the hearthstone lags the father, Musing o'er the days gone by.

Days which saw him glad and hearty, Punctual at his work of love; When the week's end brought him plenty, And he thanked the Lord above.

When his wages, earned so justly, Gave him clothing, home, and food; When his wife, with fond caresses, Blessed his heart, so kind and good.

Neat and clean each Sunday saw them, In their place of prayer and praise, Little dreaming that the morrow Piteous cries for help would raise.

Weeks roll on, and still yon chimney Gives of better times no sign; Men by thousands cry for labour, Daily cry, and daily pine.

Now the things, so long and dearly Prized before, are pledged away; Clock and Bible, marriage-presents, Both must go--how sad to say!

Charley trots to school no longer, Nelly grows more pale each day; Nay, the baby's shoes, so tiny, Must be sold, for bread to pay.

They who loathe to be dependent Now for alms are forced to ask Hard is mill-work, but, believe me, Begging is the bitterest task.

Soon will come the doom most dreaded, With a horror that appals; Lo! before their downcast faces Grimly stare the workhouse walls.

Stranger, if these sorrows touch you, Widely bid your bounty flow; And assist my poor endeavours To relieve this load of woe.

Let no more the smokeless chimneys Draw from you one word of praise; Think, oh, think upon the thousands Who are moaning out their days.

Rather pray that peace, soon bringing Work and plenty in her train, We may see these smokeless chimneys Blackening all the land again.

1862.

*

THE MILL-HAND'S PETITION.

The following verses are copied from "Lancashire Lyrics," edited by John Harland, Esq., F.S.A. They are extracted from a song "by some 'W.C.,' printed as a street broadside, at Ashton-under-Lyne, and sung in most towns of South Lancashire."

We have come to ask for assistance; At home we've been starving too long; An' our children are wanting subsistence; Kindly aid us to help them along.

CHORUS.

For humanity is calling; Don't let the call be in vain; But help us; we're needy and falling; And God will return it again.

War's clamour and civil commotion Has stagnation brought in its train; And stoppage bring with it starvation, So help us some bread to obtain.
 For humanity is calling. The American war is still lasting; Like a terrible nightmare it leans On the breast of a country, now fasting For cotton, for work, and for means.And humanity is calling.

*

CHEER UP A BIT LONGER. {2} BY SAMUEL LAYCOCK.

Cheer up a bit longer, mi brothers i' want, There's breeter days for us i' store; There'll be plenty o' tommy an' wark for us o' When this 'Merica bother gets o'er. Yo'n struggled reet nobly, an' battled reet hard, While things han bin lookin' so feaw; Yo'n borne wi' yo're troubles and trials so long, It's no use o' givin' up neaw.

Feight on, as yo' han done, an' victory's sure, For th' battle seems very nee won, Be firm i' yo're sufferin', an' dunno give way; They're nowt nobbut ceawards'at run. Yo' know heaw they'n praised us for stondin' so firm, An' shall we neaw stagger an' fo? Nowt o'th soart;--iv we nobbut brace up an' be hard, We can stond a bit longer, aw know.

It's hard to keep clemmin' an' starvin' so long; An' one's hurt to see th' little things fret, Becose there's no buttercakes for 'em to eat; But we'n allus kept pooin' thro' yet. As bad as toimes are, an' as feaw as things look, We're certain they met ha' bin worse; We'n had tommy to eat, an' clooas to put on; They'n only bin roughish, aw know.

Aw've begged on yo' to keep up yo're courage afore, An' neaw let me ax yo' once moor; Let's noan get disheartened, there's hope for us yet, We needn't dispair tho' we're poor. We cannot expect it'll allus be foine; It's dark for a while, an' then clear; We'n mirth mixed wi' sadness, an' pleasure wi' pain, An' shall have as long as we're here.

This world's full o' changes for better an' wur, An' this is one change among th' ruck; We'n a toime o' prosperity,--toime o' success, An' then we'n a reawnd o' bad luck. We're baskin' i' sunshine, at one toime o'th day, At other toimes ceawerin' i'th dark; We're sometoimes as hearty an' busy as owt, At other toimes ill, an' beawt wark.

Good bless yo'! mi brothers, we're nobbut on th' tramp, We never stay long at one spot; An' while we keep knockin' abeawt i' this world, Disappointments will fall to eawer lot: So th' best thing we can do, iv we meon to get thro', Is to wrastle wi' cares as they come; We shall feel rayther tired,--but let's never heed that,-- We can rest us weel when we get whoam.

Cheer up, then, aw say, an' keep hopin' for th' best, An' things 'll soon awter, yo'll see; There'll be oceans o' butties for Tommy an' Fred, An' th' little un perched on yo're knee. Bide on a bit longer, tak' heart once ogen, An' do give o'er lookin' so feaw; As we'n battled, an' struggled, an' suffered so long, It's no use o' givin' up neaw.

FRETTIN'.
(From "Phases of Distress--Lancashire Rhymes.")

BY JOSEPH RAMSBOTTOM.

Fro' heawrs to days--a dhreary ngth-- Fro' days to weeks one idle stons, An' slowly sinks fro' pride an' strength To weeny heart an' wakely honds; An' still one hopes, an' ever tries To think 'at better days mun come; Bo' th' sun may set, an' th' sun may rise,-- No sthreak o' leet one finds a-whoam.

Aw want to see thoose days again, When folk can win whate'er they need; O God! to think 'at wortchin' men Should be poor things to pet an' feed! There's some to th' Bastile han to goo, To live o'th rates they'n help'd to pay; An' some get "dow" {3} to help 'em through; An' some are taen or sent away.

What is there here, 'at one should live, Or wish to live, weigh'd deawn wi' grief, Through weary weeks an' months, 'at give Not one short heawr o' sweet relief? A sudden plunge, a little blow, Would end at once mi' care an' pain! An' why noa do't?--for weel aw know Aw's lose bo' ills, if nowt aw gain.

An' why noa do't? It ill 'ud tell O' thoose wur laft beheend, aw fear; It's wring, at fust, to kill mysel', It's wring to lyev mi childer here. One's like to tak' some thowt for them-- Some sort o' comfort one should give; So one mun bide, an' starve, an' clem, An' pine, an' mope, an' fret, an' live.

TH' SHURAT WEAVER'S SONG. {4}
BY SAMUEL LAYCOCK.

TUNE--"Rory O'More."

Confound it! aw ne'er wur so woven afore; My back's welly brocken, mi fingers are sore; Aw've been starin' an' rootin' amung this Shurat, Till aw'm very near getten as bloint as a bat.

Aw wish aw wur fur enough off, eawt o'th road, For o' weavin' this rubbitch aw'm getten reet sto'd; Aw've nowt i' this world to lie deawn on but straw, For aw've nobbut eight shillin' this fortnit to draw.

Neaw, aw haven't mi family under mi hat; Aw've a woife and six childer to keep eawt o' that; So aw'm rayther amung it just neaw, yo may see-- Iv ever a fellow wur puzzle't, it's me! Iv aw turn eawt to steal, folk'll co' me a thief; An' aw conno' put th' cheek on to ax for relief; As aw said i' eawr heawse t'other neet to mi wife, Aw never did nowt o' this mak' i' my life.

O dear! iv yon Yankees could nobbut just see, Heaw they're clemmin' an' starvin' poor weavers loike me, Aw think they'd soon sattle their bother, an' strive To send us some cotton to keep us alive.

There's theawsan's o' folk, just i'th best o' their days, Wi' traces o' want plainly sin i' their faze; An' a futur afore 'em as dreary an' dark; For, when th' cotton gets done, we's be o' eawt o' wark.

We'n bin patient an' quiet as lung as we con; Th' bits o' things we had by us are welly o' gone; Mi clogs an' mi shoon are both gettin' worn eawt, An' my halliday clooas are o' gone "up th' speawt!"

Mony a time i' my days aw've sin things lookin' feaw, But never as awkard as what they are neaw; Iv there isn't some help for us factory folk soon, Aw'm sure 'at we's o' be knock'd reet eawt o' tune.

*

GOD HELP THE POOR. {5}
BY SAMUEL BAMFORD.

God help the poor, who in this wintry morn, Come forth of alleys dim and courts obscure; God help yon poor, pale girl, who droops forlorn, And meekly her affliction doth endure!

God help the outcast lamb! she trembling stands, All wan her lips, and frozen red her hands; Her mournful eyes are modestly down cast, Her night-black hair streams on the fitful blast; Her bosom, passing fair, is half reveal'd, And oh! so cold the snow lies there congeal'd; Her feet benumb'd, her shoes all rent and worn;-- God help thee, outcast lamb, who stand'st forlorn!
God help the poor!

God help the poor! an infant's feeble wail Comes from yon narrow gate-way! and behold A female crouching there, so deathly pale, Huddling her child, to screen it from the cold!-- Her vesture scant, her bonnet crush'd and torn; A thin shawl doth her baby dear enfold. And there she bides the ruthless gale of morn, Which almost to her heart hath sent its cold! And now she sudden darts a ravening look, As one with new hot bread comes past the nook; And, as the

tempting load is onward borne, She weeps. God help thee, hapless one forlorn!
God help the poor!

God help the poor! Behold yon famish'd lad No shoes, no hose, his wounded feet protect; With limping gait, and looks so dreamy-sad, He wanders onward, stopping to inspect Each window, stored with articles of food; He yearns but to enjoy one cheering meal. Oh! to his hungry palate, viands rude Would yield a zest the famish'd only feel! He now devours a crust of mouldy bread-- With teeth and hands the precious boon is torn, Unmindful of the storm which round his head Impetuous sweeps. God help thee, child forlorn
God help the poor! God help the poor! Another have I found A bow'd and venerable man is he; His slouched hat with faded crape is bound, His coat is gray, and threadbare, too, I see; "The rude winds" seem to "mock his hoary hair;" His shirtless bosom to the blast is bare. Anon he turns, and casts a wistful eye, And with scant napkin wipes the blinding spray; And looks again, as if he fain would spy Friends he hath feasted in his better day Ah! some are dead, and some have long forborne To know the poor; and he is left forlorn!
God help the poor!

God help the poor who in lone valleys dwell, Or by far hills, where whin and heather grow Theirs is a story sad indeed to tell! Yet little cares the world, nor seeks to know The toil and want poor weavers undergo. The irksome loom must have them up at morn; They work till worn-out nature will have sleep; They taste, but are not fed. Cold snow drifts deep Around the fireless cot, and blocks the door; The night-storm howls a dirge o'er moss and moor! And shall they perish thus, oppress'd and lorn? Shall toil and famine hopeless still be borne!-- No! GOD will yet arise, and HELP THE POOR!

*

TICKLE TIMES.
BY EDWIN WAUGH.

Neaw times are so tickle, no wonder One's heart should be deawn i' his shoon, But, dang it, we munnot knock under To th' freawn o' misfortin to soon; Though Robin looks fearfully gloomy, An' Jamie keeps starin' at th' greawnd, An' thinkin' o'th table 'at's empty, An' th' little things yammerin' reawnd.

Iv a mon be both honest an' willin', An' never a stroke to be had, An' clemmin' for want ov a shillin',-- It's likely to make him feel sad; It troubles his heart to keep seein' His little brids feedin' o'th air; An' it feels very hard to be deein', An' never a mortal to care.

But life's sich a quare bit o' travel,-- A warlock wi' sun an' wi' shade,-- An' then, on a bowster o' gravel, They lay'n us i' bed wi' a spade; It's no use o' peawtin' an' fratchin'; As th' whirligig's twirlin' areawn'd, Have at it again; an' keep scratehin', As lung as your yed's upo' greawnd.

Iv one could but feel i'th inside on't, There's trouble i' every heart; An' thoose that'n th' biggest o'th pride on't, Oft leeten o'th keenest o'th smart. Whatever may chance to come to us, Let's patiently hondle er share,-- For there's mony a fine suit o' clooas That covers a murderin' care.

There's danger i' every station, I'th palace, as weel as i'th cot; There's hanker i' every condition, An' canker i' every lot; There's folk that are weary o' livin', That never fear't hunger nor cowd; An' there's mony a miserly crayter 'At's deed ov a surfeit o' gowd.

One feels, neaw 'at times are so nippin', A mon's at a troublesome schoo', That slaves like a horse for a livin', An, flings it away like a foo; But, as pleasur's sometimes a misfortin, An' trouble sometimes a good thing,-- Though we liv'n o'th floor, same as layrocks, We'n go up, like layrocks, to sing.

THE END

Footnotes:

{1} These stanzas are extracted, by permission, from the second volume of "Lancashire Lyrics," edited by John Harland, Esq., F.S.A. "They were written by a lady in aid of the Relief Fund. They were printed on a card, and sold, principally at the railway stations. Their sale there, and elsewhere, is known to have realised the sum of 160 pounds. Their authoress is the wife of Mr Serjeant Bellasis, and the only daughter of the late William Garnett, Esq. of Quernmore Park and Bleasdale, Lancashire."--Notes in "Lancashire Lyrics."

{2} From "Lancashire Lyrics," edited by John Harland, Esq., F.S.A.

{3} Dole; relief from charity.

{4} "During what has been well named 'The Cotton Famine,' amongst the imports of cotton from India, perhaps the worst was that denominated 'Surat,' from the city of that name in the province of Guzerat, a great cotton district. Short in staple, and often rotten, bad in quality, and dirty in condition, (the result too often of dishonest packers,) it was found to be exceedingly difficult to work up; and from its various defects, it involved considerable deductions, or 'batings,' for bad work, from the spinners' and weavers' wages. This naturally led to a general dislike of the Surat cotton, and to the application of the word 'Surat' to designate any inferior article. One action was tried at the assizes, the offence being the applying to the beverage of a particular brewer the term of 'Surat beer.' Besides the song given above, several others were written on the subject. One called 'Surat Warps,' and said to be the production of a Rossendale rhymester, (T. N., of Bacup,) appeared in Notes and Queries of June 3, 1865, (third series, vol. vii., p. 432,) and is there stated to be a great favourite amongst the old 'Deyghn Layrocks,' (Anglice, the 'Larks of Dean,' in the forest of Rossendale,) 'who sing it to one of the easy-going psalm-tunes with much gusto.' One verse runs thus:-

" 'I look at th' yealds, and there they stick; I ne'er seen the like sin' I wur wick! What pity could befall a heart, To think about these hard-sized warps!'

Another song, called 'The Surat Weyver,' was written by William Billington of Blackburn. It is in the form of a lament by a body of Lancashire weavers, who declare that they had

" 'Borne what mortal man could bear, Affoore they'd weave Surat.'

But they had been compelled to weave it, though

" 'Stransportashun's not as ill As weyvin rotten Su'.'

The song concludes with the emphatic execration, " 'To hell wi' o' Surat!'"

--Note in "Lancashire Lyrics," vol. ii., edited by John Harland, Esq., F.S.A.

{5} These beautiful lines, by the veteran Samuel Bamford, of Harperhey, near Manchester, author of "Passages in the Life of a Radical," &c., are copied from the new and complete edition of his poems, entitled "Homely Rhymes, Poems, and Reminiscences," published by Alexander Ireland & Co., Examiner and Times Office, Pall Mall, Manchester. Price 3s. 6d., with a portrait of the author.

Printed in Poland
by Amazon Fulfillment
Poland Sp. z o.o., Wrocław